T0148181

The Scarlet Letter D

How to Bounce Back from Divorce and Redefine Yourself

Jørgen Rune

ARCHWAY PUBLISHING

Scripture taken from the King James Version of the Bible.

Archway Publishing books may be ordered through booksellers or by contacting:

Archway Publishing
1663 Liberty Drive
Bloomington, IN 47403
www.archwaypublishing.com
1 (888) 242-5904

ISBN: 978-1-4808-6479-5 (sc)
ISBN: 978-1-4808-6478-8 (e)

Library of Congress Control Number: 2018907492

Print information available on the last page.

Archway Publishing rev. date: 06/25/2018

Contents

Prologue

Something felt "off" today. Something felt different. It felt – weird. Like I was losing or had lost something. Something meaningful. Something valuable. Something worth holding on to at least, I initially thought.

She was slipping. Slipping on a slope that would take her in a different direction than I was headed; till divorce do us part.

When you love someone, the unseen, strongly felt 'connection' that exists between you two can comfort you, and can warn you. What I learned about deciphering between comforting and warning is this; "warnings" can be misunderstood and misinterpreted as insecurities. I, like most headstrong men, feel insecurity coming on internally motivate ourselves. I conjure up a little mini inner-pep talk to stroke my male ego then, when I feel that insecure moment has passed, I go on about my way. However, when this particularly misinterpreted "insecurity" presented itself, I ignored it for as long as I could, until I totally dismissed it.

Bad idea. When I started dismissing my little inclinations, these insecurities, I shut them out. I didn't think that my marriage would take the sadistic turn that it inevitably did. And, by ignoring and even "sweeping under the rug" these warnings, the unexpected tidal-wave came crashing down on me and my young children. The exact day I refer to was lost in the otherwise romantic and love-sick month of February 2011. This year, by the mere mention of it would shatter my consciousness and send me into the proverbial spiral of self-loathing and bitter compunction. I was headed straight for a divorce.

That moment, when you know it's just out of your reach, (provided the actual act of reaching is taking place)you may think the spirit may be willing, but the flesh is weak. You might be one of those who was an actual witness of your ex in either *The Act,* or an act of why you are now considering a divorce. You may be one of those who found out the shattering news from an acquaintance, shared friends or parent. I was one of those who heard from incendiary sources coworkers, and other friends of friends.

The Scarlet Letter "D"

There is nothing quite like that moment. That stark realization. The second that the emotional jackhammer hits you and punches you repeatedly. Except the blade is laced with liquid nitrogen. And they both cut like a machete. You absolutely feel every sabotaging emotion, every lucid sensation. The pain is joined by a similar, but ice-cold piercing sensation of betrayal. If your heart, accompanied by your stomach, could somehow sink further than your feet, it would. But it doesn't, because obviously it's not physically possible. Would that there was some sort of panacea for those of us who begin this journey of betrayal, recovery and emotional damage control all alone. ***Which is the point and purpose and ultimate directive of this book. Page by turning page, though it may not be universally healing to everyone, just so that it provides some sort of comfort, vindication, relief and direction away from the self-loathing and misery that breaking up and divorce inevitably produces, then these words will have served their purpose.

I am reluctant to label the primary or any auxiliary functions of this book, because in so doing would limit its potential. This book may be exactly what the doctor ordered for some, and even most of the readers. Some people will receive it just as good divorce advice. There are so many angles, and so many facets that this book can and should accomplish that it's going to be different for everyone. Now with that said, walk with me.***

The day I arrived at the glaring realization I was going to start the divorce process, I was driven to a panicked uncertainty that I couldn't be more unfamiliar with. Rallying around me, my immediate family and their spouses witnessed the transforming of what earlier was a confused, scared and emotional married man into a depressed, snowball of anxiety.

The timeline is not important. Suffice to say, like most victims in an abusive relationship, I lived for two years in a Marriage Prison Camp complete with emotional bondage, mental tyranny and no intimacy. And I was devastated because my "punishment" was now over.

Most people who live in bad relationships and/or marriages often don't know they are in bad situations. They lose themselves trying to become someone the other spouse can love. I want to address how this is a very unhealthy state of mind and why the other spouse in this instance can be classified or characterized as an "emotionally abusive" spouse. As I would rehearse stories of my mistreatment and experiences to my family, enduring what I thought was just a rough patch in my marriage. It proved I was a little slow to recognize the writing was on the wall. This writing just looked like disorderly hieroglyphics on the wall to me, with no way of translating the unseen story from my distracted perspective.

People will say that ignorance is bliss, but in cases like this my ignorance was a disabling adversary. While my family was helping me translate my situation and helping me to emotionally and mentally digest my own emotions, I was hit like a defensive back cracking into an unsuspecting slot receiver across the middle of a football field. Or, for some of you that are not familiar with sports analogies, it hit me like the Titanic colliding with its dooming iceberg. Although by physical comparison, the metaphor does not measure up, the unseen and apparent impact felt as identical as it could emotionally and mentally to me. At least at first, it sure left the equivalent emotional scarring and emotional damage on an equally "Titanic" level.

I'll never forget the scene: I was standing in my parent's kitchen. Pacing around a little 7 x 10 circumference area, when the reality hit. I was so overcome with emotion, it filled my every sense and every fiber of my physical being It weakened my spirit and weakened my knees. Luckily, I was gripping the edge of the countertop because when my knees gave out, I collapsed right in front of everyone. Now imagine with me if you will; think of the absolute worst cry you've ever endured. Tears dripping down your face like leaky faucets, blood and emotions rush to your face causing it to be so red and so infuriating that you can give new meaning to the term "weeping and wailing and gnashing of teeth". My first real breath after that was arduous. I exhaled with a high-pitched wheeze, my eyes sealed shut by the tears streaming down my face and I exhaled until I absolutely had no more breath left in my lungs. Then my body somehow locked up. At the same time, I was somehow okay. I didn't pass out (at least to my knowledge). I still was aware of where I was, yet I didn't care at all where I was. I didn't care with whom I was with and I most certainly didn't care who was watching. Then, finally, my lungs filled up with air, as

I breathed in deep, still with tears streaming down my face only now accompanied by a throbbing headache and not looking forward to the next exhalation. At this point, I'm still hunched over, hands still gripping the countertop as if I'm hanging off a 1000-foot cliff. I just wanted to disappear into oblivion. I didn't want to exist. If this is the pain I had to endure, if this was the emotion I had to pass through, then I'm out! When one is finally brought to that breaking point, they may experience a rush of emotions and not fully adequately able to process, let alone decipher. They can range from rage to anxiety to depression and every color and shade of emotion in between. Lather, rinse, repeat.

Fortunately, all that personal pain and anguish wasn't for naught. Pain and suffering has a very distinct and unique way of somehow slowing down time. There's nothing comforting or easy about it. It has been my personal experience that going through pain of any kind and of any degree prepares us to receive the consequent blessing. For instance: say we know we want to increase our humility and patience so we pray, or wish (perhaps a combination of both) for humility and patience. But what we end up getting is patience and humility building experiences!

After I endured that torturous, soul suffocating experience, something happened. Something changed within me. I was free. I somehow felt liberated from the emotional cesspool that was in my head and how I perceived my marriage. In retrospect, it was as if exacerbating through that pain, torture, and emotional destruction that I had just endured, freed something. As if I had exercised demons of some sort. Not that I was possessed in any way. Not like one would see in the artificially inflated Hollywood movies. But freed in that the former dark spirit or dark entity no longer had power over me to control my thoughts or emotions. Before this experience, I had numbers of friends and family almost confront me to ask how I was doing. It wasn't in a casual social setting of a traditional "Hi-Goodbye" type of a setting necessarily, but in an attitude of them putting their hand on my shoulder, expressing genuine concern for my personal well-being. I was too ashamed and too prideful enough at the same time to assure inquiring parties that everything was above board, and that the Mrs. and I were just going through a rough patch like all couples do. I dismissed any of the glaringly obvious symptoms I was unknowingly demonstrating from those who knew me better and those who genuinely cared. Looking back on it now, I wish I wouldn't have been so prideful and arrogant. Despite my spirit and emotions feeling like I was battered worse than a blacksmiths anvil. I was in denial.

After my soul finally finished processing all those emotions, I was liberated at once! And by liberated, I mean, that I was no longer under the spell of my relationships manipulations. See, there was a point in my relationship where I did anything I could to please my spouse even to the point of losing myself and who I was as a man. Now that's not to confuse the fact that you should be willing to do anything for your spouse as they should you. However, in my mind, heart and soul were trapped in an isolated sphere of illusions and distortions designed to confuse and hurt me, eventually leading to my ultimate self-destruction if I didn't do something constructive with them. I want to believe it wasn't any purposeful doing of my former wife, but rather a weakness which was discovered in me by the adversary. That's one of the dangerous tactics of the adversary (aren't they all?), that he has so many tools in his arsenal designed to confuse, hurt, distort, and eventually destroy the hearts and spirits of man. As time has progressed over the centuries, his weapons have grown more sophisticated more elaborate, inflicting more and more damage with every attempt and every successful blow. His primary target? Families. Especially eternal families. Napoleon Bonaparte had it right: "Divide, and conquer." If Satan can divide a family, then he can use multiple fronts tactics and multiple weapons against one individual and/or their family. This tactic works more often than we are willing to admit to and face that fact. I will venture the opinion that perhaps Mr. Bonaparte was perhaps a little inspired by the Dark Prince with that tactic. Maybe he was just that good of a military mind? Consider the alternative: if a husband and wife committed to each other, stood up for each other, had each other's backs, and most importantly had each other's best interest primarily at the forefront of their mind, Satan doesn't stand a chance. Fortunately, we have a release, an "eject button" if you will. We can be bailed out by the power of the Holy Ghost at any time. Our weapon to counter the adversary's arsenal? Obedience. Plain, simple, cliché, Sunday school-standard answer, *obedience*. James E. Talmage once astutely observed:

> "Obedience to the law is the habit of the free man, it's the transgressor who fears the law, for he brings upon himself depravation, and restraint. Not *because* of the law, which would have protected him in his freedom, but because of his own rejection of law."

The direction and scope in which this quote is relevant to shoots off in all directions and applies to almost every principle in life and in this specific case, relationships and breakups and ultimately divorce. If we could all just apply this vital antidote of living disciplined and principled lives and constantly adhere to the best marital and family principles and practices, well let's just say divorces wouldn't be more numerous than marriages!

How It All Started

We've all done things we've regretted. We've all messed up an otherwise ideal, mistake-free opportunity. What I would come to know in the days and weeks and months ahead was that my marriage (the same one my then wife would almost dismissively joke about) wasn't as picture perfect as I once imagined. There will be a reoccurring theme that I will announce here and now, it is that of *agency*. It's a hard lesson to learn. Albeit one that I that I needed to learn more in-depth, despite my sincerest efforts, though not from lack of trying. Enter: MORTALITY. Nothing can prepare anyone for divorce. I am personally unaware of any classes (college, support groups, etc.,) or other that can dutifully and adequately prepare one for facing that life-altering, eternally-changing series of events.

It's daunting. It's fearful. It's scary. It's liberating. It's galvanizing. It's motivating. It's unlike any experience anyone can ever plan for, or properly execute. It's far more easily said, or in this case, read, than done. I know; I wish they had an "app" for it too.

We all suffer from insecurities in one way or another. They can have a haunting effect. Sure, we can mentally displace them, sweeping them under the proverbial rug and ignore them. But that doesn't make us what we are. We're imperfect, holistic, impractical, unreasonable, flattering and genuine. Well, at least we have good intentions while doing so, right?

Agency is likely one of the most profound gifts that we a mortals have been endowed with. It's literally our choice to decide. To become. To fall. Or, to rise.

Let me be clarion clear that I do not advocate divorce. The following words in this diatribe aren't intended to promote, facilitate, enable, or otherwise encourage divorce in any way. This collection of predicates are better meant for guidelines to divorce than any kind of rulebook may provide – provided there *is* any such a rulebook.

The "D" in the book title stands for "Divorce". Why the reference "The Scarlet Letter"? Those of us that bear the mantle of "Divorced" can often feel alienated, and ostracized. We may get the impression that we're subjected to a form of public scrutiny (oftentimes self-imposed) that the otherwise faithful Christians who still have their original family unit intact and are allowed (in so many words) to judge, to question and wonder "what happened to them?" or, even worse: "what's WRONG with them?". It's as though some, if not all of us divorcee's can read non-divorced persons minds or even hear their thoughts. Or maybe it's those insecurities relentlessly creeping in.

Divorce in any community is unfriendly to its participants. In my attempt to 'clear the smog' with the perpetual understanding and even misunderstandings about the process and pain-staking sequence of events that divorce in the Christian Faith brings to the lives of those that dare to undertake the scrutiny, and the embarrassment and overall humiliation of a Christian Divorce. And I was about to join that self-loathing clique. Despite my sincerest efforts, and though not from lack of trying to avoid such a company of people, all paths lead there, and the metaphorical river in which I was drifting on, was picking up speed. For all intents and purposes, I was on an undeviating course, headed straight for the precipice of a drop that where what once was a family, is now a family divided. Where an unspeakable number of jagged emotional and mental rocks seemingly waiting for me at the end of my fall.

Suddenly, I hate gravity. Emotional gravity to be more specific. It's just the worst. True, there are those that may tuck their tail and seek an alternative brand of solace and otherwise a worldly and artificially inflated version of peace by withdrawing from their Christian brothers and sisters. They abandon their "spiritual posts", and covenants as it were, and sprint their way to the join others in their perpetual "dancing around the Golden Calf" (circa Moses and the Ten Commandments) perhaps as to avoid and/or find relief from familial and societal judgments and even confrontations from those friends and relatives whose intentions might just be to get a more-clear picture as to the marital "falling out" and subsequent divorce.

The reasons for a Christian divorce are so diverse and often viewed by the "respondent" spouse as not that big of a deal. Filing for divorce of an otherwise malcontent spouse and then try to "work things out" as if the papers served are some sort of "wake-up call" can and does often happen. Oft times, marriages are in fact saved, and this is a good thing! The fewer divorces our society endures, and the people *in* our society endure, the better we will be as a society. Sometimes it takes the wrong type of motivation to initiate a course of action to obtain the desired results.

An example of what I mean by this is that often time people will simply follow the commandments because they don't want to face the disciplinary process, or even face the daunting process to repent for a choice that would have fragmented a portion of their character against the commandments. This is not the best form of motivation, but it certainly can be a platform to the next step of developing righteous desires. The real reason why we should keep the commandments and not indulge in any kind of sin is because we love the Lord. We are disciples of Jesus Christ, and as such, He has instructed us that if we love Him, we do so most effectively by keeping his commandments. Now, avoiding certain sins because we fear or don't want to endure the repercussions or the aftermath of the consequences is adequate, but not the totality of divine intent. It's all about our character, when all is said and done. Who we *become*. Sometimes we must take a step, in this case, "step 1a" in order to get to "step two".

Then there's the other side of filing for divorce, which is much less merciful. It's literally the point of no return. To the petitioning spouse, it's a statement that there really is no turning back on. It's the *ultimate* break-up.

I did not come about my decision for my divorce easily. Not at all. It was single-handedly the most difficult decision I have ever had to make. All by myself. Alone. Solo. I emphasize that as much as I do because of the implications that surround it. My immediate family offered plenty of support in the decision-making process. I kept hearing rhetoric along the lines that it *was* (after all) *my* decision, which, at the time, was hard to hear, let alone act on. Maybe it was a result of subconscious conditioning from my shrapnel-riddled marriage that caused me to think that I was virtually incapable of *making* this decision. As a direct result, I was so used to not wanting any friction by never disagreeing or offering a difference of opinion and/or view to the tyrannical order that I later discovered was my marriage. I was afraid to make the decision, any decision, for that matter. I was afraid to carry out the execution of this all-to-critical decision to try and either live in a marriage that I wasn't happy in and just "stick it out" for my two kids, or be the bold man I once was and throw the ultimate break-up literature at my then wife, and start the process of rebuilding myself. It wasn't until I was -what I refer to as- "emotionally vomiting" on my only brother (of whom, is one of the smartest and most logical humans on this fair planet) he stopped me mid-vomit and lovingly and sternly confronted me with a voice of reason that I will ever remember. He said: "This is a choice YOU have to make. I can't and won't make it for you and neither will anyone else. Consider the alternative if one of us (meaning my immediate family) told you to get a divorce then you do it and it ends up being the wrong choice. You then can blame whoever gave you that advice! I don't want that responsibility, nor does anyone else!"

That line of logic and pure reasoning struck a very dusty, and rarely used chord in me. The reverberations of that statement resonated to a chord that was somehow apparently attached to my decision-making and reasoning capabilities. Which reminds me that the cliché "Happy wife = happy life" needs to be so carefully articulated and executed. Spouses who will walk all over their mates even to the extent of emasculating or defeminizing them in public and privately, just to get their way are not in a healthy relationship. More like a dictatorship with marital benefits. One of many examples of "there must be opposition in all things."

"Then, what *DO* we do, author?" Some may ask. I maintain a quote by late Prophet, President Gordon B. Hinckley:

"[spouses should] have an anxious concern for the welfare of the other."

That's the best kept secret to a successful relationship and marriage right there. So, I needed a few items in my decision-making process. I need to exercise my God-given agency and make this decision *myself.*

Then, once I DO make said decision, I see it through. I get the Lords backing and stamp of approval and I move forward to executing it. I get to make a choice. All by *myself.* That daunting concept alone terrified me. It had such a paralyzing and bowel-evacuating fear attached to it, that it helped to better conceptualize my own lonely mortality and that it affected my sleep for weeks. It affected my eating habits and appetite. It affected my work. Not to mention my family life. I became reclusive. I had my basement apartment (I was separated from my then-wife at the time) and it was the perfect hideaway for my school studies and gaming activities and to pass the time (which allegedly, is supposed to heal all wounds). All in the effort to dull the pain and destructive bandwidth in my head and heart and soul over losing my wife and family.

I truly hope none of the readers of this story ever come to the decision to divorce on a whim. Your divorce (If you're considering getting one) is one of careful planning, precision and a near-surgical approach with plenty of moving pieces that you, more than likely, haven't considered all the lives this will impact. That however, shouldn't scare anyone from the prospect of divorce if that is truly the answer for your situation.

All marriages and relationships can be compared to driving on a road to a certain, mutually-happy goal decided and agreed upon by both spouses when they exchange nuptial vows. How a couple decides and then practices loving one another will immediately impact how "wide" or "narrow" their road becomes as their journey together progresses. The more reasons both husbands and wives try to find ways to love their spouse, the wider their respective road gets. Why a "wide road" some may ask? Because, anyone who has been on winding, twisting, turning-type highway (yes, I'm seeking to insert a line on how *Life is a Highway* to this wordplay and parable!) the wider the road, the more "room" there is for the correction of errors and more room for willing and eager forgiveness from both parties for the other's spouse. A happy marriage and relationship requires both spouses to be good at forgiving, empathy, and relentless loyalty. Love them how *you* would want to be loved.

Contrastingly, the more reasons the spouses look to each other with a "what have you done for me lately?" type attitude, and where both spouses actively and eagerly "keep score" is not only highly dysfunctional, but with every worthless breath of cutting the other spouse down, abusive. And abuse of any and all forms: manipulations, silent treatment, physical and emotional abuse, withholding intimacy and becoming coercive, etc., can and will further narrow the road, making potential disasters nearly inevitable, with even the slightest ill-navigated oversight.

These types of marriages and the people in them can quickly lose sight of what they signed up for in the first place. They can get seriously distracted, looking for some "strange", as it were, and will find themselves headed straight towards a marital explosion. Unfortunately, this lesson isn't learned until well after the fact, by acting out/up in one's marriage, even to the point of infidelity, *never* solves what was wrong in the first place!

In the Christian faith (and inclusively any culture & society where marriage is the standard), there has been a major shift in what some may regard as "tolerance" for the divorced faithful Christian. It has been remarkable and quite overwhelming to see the love, the outreach and the overall acceptance of us divorcee's as friends, family and ward members who have any level of stewardship involving us! Priesthood and auxiliary leadership, it seems, may have been counselled to offer support in most any unique way to assure us that we divorcee's still belong and are loved and are accepted. In a time in our lives especially, when those favorable emotions are essentially non-existent considering our current relationship status and standing.

The Decision

Commendations therefore, for all of us Saints who understand the Gospel of Jesus Christ to our respective degrees, and embrace any Saint regardless of their trials, struggles, successes and disappointments, as we are all under one roof here! We got to look out for each other! If anyone of us, Christian, of any race creed or denomination ever has the inclination to judge somebody else, we need to remember we are not their Savior, ergo we really have no right to judge anyone! Nor do they have the right to judge us. As we all have fallen short of the example of Jesus Christ and all are imperfect. We have no right to judge someone else simply because they choose to sin differently than we do (thanks, President Uchtdorf!) There are those who will argue that staying in an abusive, emotional, mental or physical or other, relationship, is far worse for yourself and your kids (if you have any) than actually executing the divorce. I'm one of them. It's been said "I'd rather be *from* a broken home than *live* in one."

There is a much different and a much more elevated life after divorce than anyone could ever imagine. I will address this in another chapter.

Of course, all things considered, we will be viewed differently than those people who choose to remain in their marriages for both the right and wrong reasons, but who cares? They have their own sets of clustered trials that are much different from ours! They don't deserve to be judged and neither do we! There are people out there who share our pain, share our excitement, share our enthusiasm for ours and each other's children, our religion and other wholesome activities. It is, for lack of a better way of putting it, an entirely new and different form of civilization with an equally strong, smart, polished, and struggling group of single persons.

This type of singles society has opened my eyes to so many possibilities and thoughts about how diverse we as a people really are! At the heart of it all, at the heart of these two entirely different family structures and civilizations we all share several different common denominators: we all want love. We all want to be loved. We all want to have someone to come home to, and we all want to be our version of "better". Perhaps most importantly, we deserve to be loved. A close friend of mine, while going through his divorce, told me in confidence that his soon-to-be ex-wife once uttered to him "You deserve to be with someone who's willing to dote on you. That person is just not me." Now, that's just cold. Like liquid nitrogen "cold". I was unashamedly heartbroken for my friend!

When God gave us agency, He also gave us the ability to create. He is, after all the Divine Creator, and how else can we practice becoming like Him if we don't have the ability to create as well? Hartman Rector Jr. explained: "[The] ability to turn everything into something good appears to be a godly characteristic. Our Heavenly Father always seems able to do this. Everything, no matter how dire, becomes a victory to the Lord. Joseph, although a slave and wholly undeserving of this fate, nevertheless remained faithful to the Lord and continued to live the commandments and made something very good of his degrading circumstances. People like this cannot be defeated" (in Conference Report, Oct. 1972, 170; or Ensign, Jan. 1973, 130).

This goes beyond creating children. This involves creating relationships, this involves creating a home where peace and love and harmony can be felt. This most importantly involves our own happiness, everybody defines happiness and measures their happiness differently. Happiness has a lot of similarities at the heart of it all. It usually always involves serving, loving, and caring for other people who are close to us and who mean something to us on both on a family, friend, professional and a divine level. Our true happiness exists. It is real, and even though abstract, it is most easily felt within. It's up to us to find it, shape it, molded, embrace it, and make it our own.

I have been blessed with a very adaptable, dynamic personality. I can blend seamlessly into most any situation. Even while facing some of the more disagreeable antics and actions by parties involved with my divorce. I discovered, much to my shame, that I had a bad habit of divulging my marital woes to miscellaneous persons in random places, almost like it was a conversation starter! It isn't - and never should be. If you find yourself emotionally vomiting on complete strangers, *Don't*! Don't be that person! Now, I say that tongue-in-cheek, squeezing as much humor in that as I can.

As I made a move to involve my family more, mainly for support in my time of melancholy, I'd petition my father for starters. Most times Dads can be great problem solvers and offer many solutions to what is normally considered a venting session! Moms and sisters and lady friends in general have a way of having great listening skills, validating our feelings and taking our side on the issues and matters at hand. Sometimes we just want to be heard. Sometimes we just want someone to listen to us and grant us a form or semblance of peace and affirmations that we are not crazy, or broken or any combination of the two!

It was again time to venture into my brother's brain to scoop up more clever advice. As with our similar juncture, I was emotionally vomiting on my brother, complaining to him some of the many struggles I had in dealing with my (almost) ex. What he told me next struck at me like a blind-side haymaker. He told me: "You *have* to wrap your head around the fact that she doesn't have your best interests at heart anymore!" (implying if she ever did). My next thoughts were: "Have I been too nice/agreeable/compliant up to this point? Have I been the proverbial "push-over" in these "give and take" scenarios? Have I…? After a quick assimilation of what I've been doing all along, to be agreeable and suddenly seeing that it had not only gotten me nowhere, but *further* away from a solution with the endgame of my divorce! I concluded that I *had* been taken for granted! Those details regarding our divorce should be more in a neutral, 50/50 give-and-take type scenario! And, *therefore* I HAD been *being* taken for granted in some of the worst most uncompromising ways and that set me off. That infuriated me! Even though I was still married, I was still totally being taken for granted. I assumed that the nicer attitude and actions towards me would be that of a caring and sympathetic (soon-to-be) ex-wife! Wrong. After I quantified that thought in my head, I then realized I needed to start looking out for #2 (as my children are #1.) Because no one else would. And no one else was.

It's never an easy transition going from loving someone, caring about them, their thoughts, their wishes and their desires, to basically converting your thoughts and emotional disposition into now regarding your former loved one as "Public Enemy #1". I will tell you now, hating them or wishing them ill is not the right attitude, easiest one it may be, but it's too detrimental. Here's why: For a lot of us who go through any form of betrayal from a spouse the first emotional reaction is to resent, despise, dislike and even loathe them. Note, that I did not use the word "hate" in my list of adjectives. I personally feel that the word is overused, and even used indiscriminately, to the point that it's lost its meaning. In any case, they are not your enemy. They may do and say and act in enemy ways, but they are *still* your children's parent. They still have close ties with us. We may not like it and may go against every physical fiber in our gut, body and heart, and it won't be easy to muster, but they deserve still to be treated like a loved one just going through a very hard time. We don't have to support them in all their decisions, especially if they're detrimental to the family, but we *must* respect their decision-making ability, and their agency. No matter how many people it hurts or influences in negative ways. No matter how many people they leave in their disastrous and destructive wake.

Top questions to ask oneself about if divorce is, or is not the correct solution for you:

1) Is/Are your reasons for considering/wanting a divorce selfish, or beneficial for those in your immediate family?
2) If you get divorced, will that solve the surrounding problems?
3) Will it make the surrounding problems worse?
4) If you get a divorce, will you be happier or more sad?
5) Are you prepared to live life as a single person again? A single parent (if applicable)?
6) Are you or your partner at all willing to work things out via counselling, compromise, or other recommended means necessary to heal your marriage?
7) Do you or your partner even want to save/salvage your marriage?

Alone Again

There's nothing quite like that moment when you feel like you have nothing and no one. It lingers, and as a direct result, it can get very dark in one's mind very fast. But this wasn't necessarily bad in this case. Some of you might ask how that could be? That's the thing about the dark side, it has its own way of molding you to *your* own benefit. This is a delicate balance, otherwise we run the risk of losing ourselves and our agency to the darkness. I always knew I had a choice as to how every situation and every circumstance could define me. If your wherewithal is where it needs to be, you can sense it. It's also a lot of how I let each situation affect me, and how I allowed it to change me as a result. It's true; the dark side can overpower us, *if we let it*. That is a real big "if". There are also plenty of lessons to be learned from the moments of darkness in our lives. These lessons are all tailored and customized to what we need in that moment and in that time in our lives.

I came to the crossroads of: "Will I use this moment as a stepping stone, or a stumbling block?" How I respond to that question will determine my eventual destiny. I'll either ascend, or descend. Either grow, or weaken. I can build strength of character, or lose myself to the darkness. There's no middle ground. No "in between". It's either progress, or perish. When I would go through the various emotional storms, they would reveal their intensity either too soon, that I wasn't properly prepared for them, and/or too late as I was already in the "thick" of it and was scrambling to get myself in order. Whether it was the emotional equivalent to Tsunamis, Tropical Storms, Jet Streams, Tornado's in all their different ferocities, I'd welcome the Hurricanes of trials in my life. I would only later learn that in the best of ways, they are the defining moments that shape and mold me in one of two outcomes: Either I drew further away from any light and spirituality, including the source of it. All the while, being tempted to blame God for my poor spiritual countenance and brazen attitude toward my life's status quo. Or, I finally came around to the tender knowledge that I'm in control of my destiny, and whatever God throws at me, I'm going to use my best current spiritual skill set to swing away at every single trial and storm like a blind man with a lightsaber! There's nothing pleasant about it, as it is a process and quite the grind. It's not meant to be a quick fix. There's just no way that could work or would work. Timing and preparation have everything to do with it. Timing is essential because I came to discover that time and tide wait for no man (or woman). It basically forced me to adapt and become adaptable in the future. This was equally imperative, as nothing stays the same for long - not too long, anyway. President Ezra Taft Benson once stated: "When you choose to follow Christ, you choose to be changed." Change, or fall behind. Progress or perish, as I have aforementioned.

Preparation is critical because there's no time like the present! I could not and cannot afford to *not* be ready for the right moment to act, or be acted upon. Cousin to "timing", my preparation can define my moments of truth. As these moments were, and are going to come at me whether I'm ready or not. So, might as well be ready. If I'm not ready, then I run the risk of not only losing some very critical blessings. But I may also miss the moment. The moment that, if I metaphorically blink, then I'll run the risk of missing some opportunistic change, some pivotal moment that could have set in motion an entirely different and chain of events. The old cliché applies: "You only get what you give." If you give everything, you get everything. If you give a little, well, you get the idea. Likely more so than we even want to acknowledge. I believe that's because those of us who find ourselves in this and other similar situations in life, i.e. dating or breakup or post-divorce, we're in a temporary state of emotional flux. An emotional and even spiritual state of limbo, as it were. We cannot and may not be able to understand the gravity of the situation until gravity's design is completely fulfilled. And we hit the wall or the ground that our tailored "disaster" is meant to force us into. In these moments of greatest uncertainty, we have a delicate opportunity to choose. Choose what, you might ask? Choose exactly *who* we are going to become and *what* we're going to allow ourselves to become as a result.

It's times like this I found the need to talk to myself. Not in some schizophrenic sense, but take some personal inventory. To find out the "why" to everything relevant to me and my poor scarred psyche (I say, tongue in cheek). Why I act this way, why I responded to certain situations the way I did. Because some forms of common sense had me believe that I was trying to escape something. Or even more dangerously, trying to create an alternate lifestyle or mentality to hide emotions and feelings I had inside; or even worse - to run away from them altogether. Even though I might mentally be able to run away from these very valid emotions, I can only run until they or I are out of sight, (as it were) and then, rest on my laurels, if I so choose. If only for a short moment. It's only a matter of time before they finally catch up to me, as they always do. Embracing and accepting these emotions and truths can be very liberating, if "taken as prescribed". It's easy to not want to "ingest" them as the initial intake can cause emotional pain and unwanted suffering. But, believe it or not, like ripping off the proverbial band aid, the initial painful pull-off will be but for a small moment. Afterwards, now that our heart and mind are initialized, we can set ourselves up for success. It's usually always like that, right? We get some resistance, some hardship before the journey, and even pushing back through the process. Two motivational phrases that work well here are:

First: Smooth waters never made a skilled sailor.

Second: Calm seas don't carry our "ships" across the ocean. Stormy seas do.

I needed to reason with myself. I needed to tell myself why I do the things I do. My first steps in this process were in the dark. It was an unfamiliar pathway that led to knowledge and experience that later became invaluable to me. However, it came at a very costly, personal hidden price. I learned in some of the worst ways that people can get seriously hurt by my actions and by the mess and size of the path in my wake, especially my closest loved ones. Because, I'll tell you what, we are really going to hate it when our actions cause our loved ones to become mad and confused. What do we want people to take away from what we do? From the bridges we burn, and from the feelings we hurt? Consider this reality: if we are totally honest with ourselves, there is no excuse for our delinquent rebellious behavior. No justified alibi. No sanctuary to seek refuge from the emotional storm we've created. There's no real defense if somebody, or multiple persons get hurt or confused by their perception of who we are. That aftermath becomes increasingly problematic, as other's perceptions become distorted by our actions. Especially by people closest to us. The ironic thing is we may initiate our socializations with pure and even innocent intentions. Meaning that most times we just wanted our audience to experience it through us. Everything that makes our partner unique. This makes perfect sense really. Because that's mostly all that us humans naturally want anyway is to be acknowledged, to be identified as one who matters to someone who matters to us. That's when appearances can get distorted. We can convince ourselves we are helping other people feel special, wanted, needed, and included, when it's actually pulling then away.

This is usually where divorce and breakups have a consistent and messed up way of putting us in a weird place emotionally while the messes just keep piling up. Sure, we can try to apologize away our actions, in hopes that the apology might be taken seriously. But the more confused we are, the more we act out, the more the messes just keep piling up. It's only a matter of time before we won't even be able to fool ourselves into knowing how many more times we can try to apologize to those effected, let alone ourselves, before even the word "apology" loses its meaning,

Christians Vs The World

One of the many problems that exists especially in today's relationships, are that the concepts and attributes of loyalty, honesty, integrity, gumption and fidelity are widely considered as "relative". Not only relative, but if one partner in any given relationship were to slip up, or have some sort of snafu, or in other words raise a "red flag" that it is somehow okay, and even tolerable. Now, the relationship dynamic suddenly shifts from an empathetic and sympathetic, patient, forgiving platform, to a now "on notice" disposition. As if spouses and relationship partners nowadays are merely an employee of sorts, that can be "Martially Terminated" if the other spouse doesn't like their other halves behavior, on any number of levels and for any given reason. When nearly every Christian relationship related doctrine would beg to differ. I'm not sure who else has noticed, but the more desensitized we, as a society become, the wider the chasm becomes between the churches standards and whatever the world standards seem to be at the time. While the church's standards are firm and immovable, the world standards, tend to look just like the foundation (or, rather *lack thereof*) the Great and Spacious building as outlined in Lehi's Dream in the Book of Mormon, stating "as if it were in the air", giving further credence to the saying, "If you don't stand for something, you'll fall for anything." To which I add, "With no foundation, it's a matter of time before one falls."

The wider the chasm, the more the church and its teachings appear to be archaic to those that follow and/or pay more attention to the trends of the world and its "circling the drain" morals. The adversary has made it so easy to get caught up in the mainstream of the media's rhetorical bravado and social media nuances with all its powerful influences. Although these are some of his strongest current devices, the Master Jesus Christ has also been revealing many ways for us children to use the same channels to unite and strengthen the kingdom of God. It's been said, almost ad nauseam, that the dark prince's greatest trick was to convince the world that he doesn't exist. I mean, think about it: How much easier is it to indulge in every physical gratification and sensation when everyone else around you seem to be so strictly disciplined with church morals? Or even just religious guidelines. And they are viewed as "so confined and so restricted" that they cannot have any kind of "fun"?

So, then the question becomes: How do we justify and rationalize being able to allow ourselves some clean with harmless indulgences? How easy is it becomes for those lines to appear blurry and then the incessant drumbeat of desensitization slowly deadens not only our physical taste buds (sensations the whole body can feel) but more *spiritually* eradicating, the taste buds of our soul? Then, unknowingly, the internal tolerance and self-discipline, or in other words, the dulled-conscience quickly erodes away. After justifications and rationalizations meet whatever rationale that we allow, they will then satisfy our physical and apparent emotional needs. So, these sensations and emotions quickly become our sabotaging allies to our own personal and inner cause of spiritual freedom from the bondage of sin. They can provide relief from our conscience. They help smooth over the otherwise rough edged, inconvenient commandments as facilitator's, enablers and profiteers. And even worse, both predators and victims sadly become desensitized to the point where they become past feeling. The only remaining restraint than becoming, how dim our dulled conscience allows.

The overarching message is that nothing good, wholesome, or spiritually strengthening, has or will ever come from tarrying with the world's "solutions".

The relieving of emotional pain, and inner turmoil of a needing, and wanting of my soul that felt so lost and adrift as I deadpanned through the toughest moments and days, weeks and months of my divorce. These temptations are never more intense. Never more present. Never more appealing. Because that's another device of the adversary to bombard his message of self-medicating, disguised as spiritual healing through physical indulgences and natural-man tendencies. His message is simply wrong. Many people fall for it, however, because it's an "easy sale" for the adversary. All it can take is for us to listen just once and become further enticed and be persuaded to the point of acceptance that "we deserve this" and only a little won't hurt". Then, we look at the world now, with its drug-drenched, salaciously-enhanced and immorally induced, spiritually damaging bravado that seems so inviting at the time. Many of us have had to learn the hard way as well. Thankfully, equally as many have also come back! Keep a watchful "spiritual eye" out, just like there are angels round about to bear us up, there are also dark entities that are just waiting for us to give up and whisper in our ear, so to speak, and drag us down to depths we never wanted to be.

Post-Marital Reflections

It was the best of times; if only someone would have told me. Like most of us, we use sarcasm as a defense mechanism to shield myself from a dark reality. A reality that I did have something good, at least somewhere in that journey. Maybe I loved her too much, or maybe sometimes not enough. But some-crazy-how, it ended up being a fatal twist of both. I knew that we had something good. Nay, even something great. But not all things great will last. Some of these great things fade away to teach us a divine lesson or two. Or to educate us for a future event. Some great things occur to spare us pain. While other great things occur that will cause us pain, so that we will grow. Pain, discomfort, and growth all have a purpose; they all serve some greater internal, personal cause. They promote spiritual, emotional, and mental growth. What younger generations may not ever fully appreciate, let alone understand or really practice about marriage, is that marriage is essentially both a legal commitment, a written commitment, with a freight-load of unwritten, under-identified promises and commitments of *unconditionally* having each other's backs.

The ideal marriage consists of two imperfect people who just straight up refuse to give up on each other. Sadly though, that kind of mental and emotional disposition takes time. Ironically, at the same time, new and young couples don't always have that vision. If you're any kind of "human", you just want it now. Some of us must scrape along, living paycheck to paycheck, hoping one day we will find our big break. But once we finally make that leap to the other side, get past all the monotony, we can realize that this is what life and matrimony has been about the whole time! Those of us that now know what I'm talking about, when I say that it means everything. Or it meant everything, to have a best friend hold your hand, give us a hug, offer us their love as a shelter and a safe-haven while life takes turns kicking both of us in the butt. It's a gentle reminder from our Heavenly Father that these tabernacles of clay (our physical bodies) are only on loan for a very short amount of time.

Then, more irony sets in. Sometimes it will be a traumatic event, some sort of mortal wake-up call that is just extreme enough for us to gain perspective and with perspective comes clarity. When the shining moments of clarity recalibrate our prospective, they can set us straight for good. But just like anything else in life, once we get used to our circumstances complacency sets in. Then, with this newfound perspective, complacency has a way of causing the distortion to come back in to our vision. Our once clarion-like glimpse with that all-too-sacred and important Eternal Perspective. What once was found, is now lost. The lines get fuzzy and distorted. The world enables many twists and turns on an already very rocky path. Be it fate, be it mortality, or any number of cosmic factors, we humans have an uncanny way of flinching at something, anything, and losing that moment; that sliver of time that possibly may have changed everything. But isn't that just the way of life?! If life was meant to be easy, if life was seamless, effortless, heck, even less filled with complexities, we would never mess up, our kids would always be safe and perfect, and we would never have any regrets, which leaves me to believe we just might spend all that time been ignorantly happy.

Now I know some of us reading this would be happy to settle for a piece of that moment in time right now! Heck, that doesn't make us bad people, it makes us human. I've certainly had those weak moments where I wish it would be taken away. Then I find myself falling into that emotional trap of replaying certain events in my mind and almost reliving outcomes that I have no control over, and I will never actually experience. This is also one of the devices of the adversary. Some of his favorite tools are regrets, remorse, shame and guilt. None of these are byproducts of God. So, I check myself. I invite you as the reader to do the same, in a way that's befitting to you. Whenever I started to feel these feelings, I have learned to recognize quickly the source of those negative feelings - then quickly cast them back to hell where they came from. Ain't nobody got time for *that!* Otherwise, you'll quickly find yourself on a spiritually-declining slippery slope. It just so happens that slippery slopes are angled downward for a reason. They are a very quick and very effective one-way trip into the very sticky mire of self-loathing and self-pity. It's a horrible place to be stuck. By the time anyone hits this very sticky sudden stop at the end of the fall, we may struggle to know how to get unstuck. The adversary had me convinced at times that I was now left to my own devices. That now I was completely and utterly abandoned. He tried mightily to convince me that even God had abandoned me, and that I was not deserving, worthy, or worth the effort to be saved. This is an obvious lie. I already know the answer to this problem. Not only was I worth it, but I <u>am</u> so much so, that I was worth God's Only Begotten Son's best efforts. Christ did what He did because He knew we couldn't. He paid a price He didn't have to pay for His brothers and sisters that would largely take Him and His best efforts for granted. Just to be thorough and fulfilling on my end, the atonement is readily available, because "His hand is stretched out still".

Alone, But not Lonely

The proverbial hammer of singlehood can hit pretty daggone hard. Even reality TV doesn't do real-life justice anymore. We've all had them. Those countless sleepless nights, of hours days weeks and months that I actually envied for the reality TV cast members (albeit) contrived trials, because at the time, they seem so much more easy and simplistic than my own. But it had a reverse effect on me. The reality TV shows helped me understand the gravity of my own situation. Which then led me to a dark place where I wondered if I would ever be an adequate or if not marginal father to my children. Considering my own set of circumstances and the tears, trials, and possible triumphs, the more realistic my failures, those are what kept me and my over-active imagination up at night till 2:00, 3:00 and some nights even 4:00 A.M., just spacing out, staring aimlessly at the ceiling. When the ceiling offered no comfort or solutions, I'd get lost in all my thoughts of what I did wrong. What did I do to cause her to respond the way she did that justified and ended up concluding to a divorce? I would have thoughts of: "Would I have changed anything? Would I take any of this cluster mess back?" It can be fun to daydream, conceptualize, and even fantasize all the numerous alternative outcomes. As if my divorce was a twisted version of a "Choose Your Own Adventure" series. If only...

When I tried to peer into the future to even imagine my children's emotions, thoughts and superficially contrived actions to tell myself anything, my heart emptied. Primarily because I just couldn't envision them taking me serious in any degree. How could they? I was this man-child, drenched with untrue accusations about me and conversely about my perception of the truth. Young children often don't realize and some adults may argue is that the teller's version of truth is always and inevitably subject to their bias and consequently their lack of information.

That's the funny thing about it truth, not only is the anecdote "perception is reality", fully realized in that cliché and almost equally redundant is it in the eyes of the beholder, but it always seems to have someone trying to outsmart it. Whether it be a form of prestidigitation, a silver tongue, or even a proverbial forked-tongue, laced with crafty efforts to twist the truth to shape, form and posture the storyteller in a greater more favorable light to its listener. Fortunately, for all parties involved, the truth will, in the end, always have its day. This fact is one of many things that I love about the truth; It is eternal and unchanging. There is no use trying to run from it and there is certainly no use trying to hide from it. The truth can be compared to the children's tale of <u>The Tortoise and the Hare.</u> The truth, personified by the Tortoise, is steadfast and consistent, whereas the hare in this example, can be any number of metaphors. Here is my very short example - the Hare will personify anything less than the truth, and well, we all know how that story ends.

Sure, gossip can travel fast amongst certain circles of friends, groups of people, even among social network platforms. True, there will even be believers of these half-truths and any version of gossip, biased or other. It is heartbreaking and equally sad that there are those among us who have eager ears practically itching to hear something less than the truth. These ignorant believers have their reasons. Any one of us can write our own chapter or two, or even write our own book about the liars in our lives. But that is neither the intent nor purpose of this book. It is a fool's errand to give any kind of voice to naysayers and those who both love and make lies. That's what we have supermarket tabloids for. Besides, once we see them for who they really are, and even if we understand for a moment, why they behaved so poorly with the information they were given, the charm has already fallen off, and they're like the Emperor's new clothes. They parade around as if they are someone or something great, and those who want to be esteemed as anything outside the popular clique, they go along praising and applauding the liars and gossipers for the façade of their "bravery". Slowly convincing themselves of their own con.

What screws us up the most in life is the picture in our head of how it's supposed to be. This is particularly true when a father (in my example) is used to a four-year-old habit of every morning waking up to the pitter-patter of little feet crawling into bed every morning. Waking him up with their cute little struggles of trying to crawl into bed with him. Then when they finally do, the gentle resonance of giggles and overall good morning loves fill the available airspace. We're reminded all over again why we are alive! In these early twilight moments in the early morning, it's oh, so real. We can wake up reaching up and towards them as if they are in front of us. This mid-dream subconscious gesture slowly fades like a mirage. When you finally come to, you're heartbreakingly saddened, as the realization and current reality now is, it's just reliving the pseudo-tangible experience, only to have it all taken away by your signature next to the signature of their mother (or father) on the same legal documents that says that your children, your life's blood and the happiness that comes every morning because they are in your life, can only now happen at dictated times and in dictated ways from now on.

There is no doubt that I am and would be lost without my children. They are my Muse. Both my children bring light back into my life. They are my cat's meow, the Apple(s) of my eye and the reason why the sun rises and sets in my tainted imperfect world. Because of them, my love only grows and I can go on living. I confess that I didn't like them very much at first. They were just these frustrating little noise makers that took time away from me wanting to be with their mom and maintain some level of physicality with their mother. What women may or may not fully realize is that after they give birth to their children, their husband (barring any legal marital situation) can feel quickly that he is being neglected and otherwise alienated. This may not happen to everyone, but, more oft than not, husbands and fathers are invited themselves to their own private Pity Party. And rightly so, I mean, babies aren't just going to take care of themselves. So, us men carry on in our wife's neglect thinking and even believing that we are, for the most part, on a very lonely island.

My children were like most babies, I guess. They smelled nice - when they didn't have a fresh-brown trout in their diaper. Even as they grew, they didn't seem to have much interest in me, which us fathers can find disingenuous. New mother's get on this emotional and physical child-focused Disneyland ride, where it's just them and their babies against the world. Funny with age, how some things never can and will not change. One day, I found myself slowly being blown away with the concept of exactly how being a parent changes you. We don't know when it hits, we just know that it does. Prior to all this, I was invincible, untouchable. Then suddenly, my heart was somehow pounding outside of my body, feeling like they were exposed to the vicious elements of wind, fire, and ice. For some intent and purposes, it was! It was a penetrating and profound realization of senses. None of us will ever know how deep and profound love is, nor how many facets and components love has until we experience and dive into all its workings. As Emerson Hart once sang: "Why can't we see that there's more to love than we will ever know?" Truer words have never been spoken or sung!

Having the profound fatherly love for them has been the most intense, yet painful growth experience of my life. In some cases, it's been almost too much to endure. Yet somehow, I remain. I still stand. As their father, I made a silent vow to protect them from the morals, (or lack thereof) deceits, confusions, and distortions of the outside world.

Dads for the smaller part (okay, the *larger* part...) can be a child in a man's body. The toys and the chores just get bigger, and on the same parallel, so do their responsibilities. Not every one of us dads embraces all these changes and responsibilities in the same way, at the same time, or even at all. We just endure them, power through them, execute them perfectly, or demonstrate a need for improvement. Welcome to mortality, right? Some dads mess up or fail to execute often enough, that their wives or significant others just grow tired of their "consistent inconsistency". Some of us just have a different learning curve, or maybe are not adequately motivated enough to dedicate all our efforts to total perfection all the time and in everything. I'm 100 percent positive that everyone reading this can relate to that statement not only personally, but perfectly. Lastly, I recall, perfection is not a prerequisite for being in a marriage or relationship. So, why do so many of us demand it from our spouse or significant other when we ourselves are so far from perfection? True, strident souls such as ourselves are fully aware that we are not perfect, so why require or even demand perfection from everyone else? Contrastingly, there are those things that spouses ought to be "perfect" in - as in maintaining marital vows of fidelity. If we have a temple marriage, then we owe it to ourselves and to our spouse and especially our children to maintain those values, promises and covenants. If said perfection was a prerequisite and or an imperative, then we have no business getting into a relationship and should maybe seek some professional counselling. Ideally, we shall cut each other and ourselves a little slack, recognize our own imperfections as well as other's imperfections and date, court, become engaged and marry for potential and the pursuit of excellence and perfection. If the pursuit of excellence and perfection is not currently motivating for anyone of us, then we should date with the intention of finding someone that will lift us up, make us be proud of who we are and achieve greatness for them and for ourselves. The key, I have found, to earthly, temporal and eternal happiness is finding someone who will continue to lift us up and us willing to continually lift them up, hand in hand, as we ascend together.

When Everything Has Changed

Can you imagine the rest of your life centered around the worst things that have happened to you? Or the perceived wrong things you have ever done? Now that is a seemingly endless and extremely depressing prospect. When we are in this final moment (and by "moment" I mean the last months, weeks and days - prior to the pending decision to divorce) and reliving all the destructive events leading up to this decision and the actual execution thereof, the gravity of *the real* sets in.

We may find ourselves funneling out certain options. If we are truly honest with ourselves, we most likely may be filtering out every reason to stay in the marriage or relationship. Slowly but surely, any rationalization to stay, mentally and/or emotionally may be deduced to absolute zero. Divorcing or breaking up also kills other options to stay. We shouldn't be, or feel guilt or pity for this emotional disposition. Divorce is rarely a cry for help; sometimes we just don't want help. It's the natural process of things.

Just don't let divorce change you into a sociopath. There's too many of these "wolves in sheep's clothing" rampaging about, destroying lives and breaking hearts and families, leaving countless other in their path of devastation. The irony of this is, they don't realize they're even doing so much damage.. They don't and can't emotionally quantify their own emotions. They're the spiritual and emotional actual manifestation of "desensitized." This again is why, yet again, agency is so critical and imperative to our decision process in everything we do, large or small.

It can be accepted that the characteristics that are least desirable in a relationship are that of of immaturity, selfishness, pride, arrogance, self-centeredness, and prudence.

Contrastingly, an individual that is ready and can be considered "relationship material" are, but not limited to: loving, giving, enduring, patient, understanding, and encouraging and supportive towards the other partner. Unfortunately, these garden-variety of characteristics are lost (for some/the most part) on these later generations of society.

Upon further reflection, the reality of our divorced and now single identity causes us to be internally, emotionally and spiritually conflicted. Right away, we may have a sense of feeling that we don't know where we fit in. Or even if we do fit in anywhere to begin with! To make matters even worse, the thought of realizing the sense of ever fitting in again, in the event we ever did. The sudden jump or perhaps an even better metaphor, being Quantum Leaped out of the "married and/or married with children" world, and then finding ourselves immediately stuck in the "divorced, newly single", and perhaps from other's perspectives: "broken, discharged, tainted, rejected, insufficient, and otherwise relationship-ly incapable" world.

Others may even encourage us to hold onto what makes us parents, or a great person, or to remain a disciple of Christ; in an effort to cover up, or bandage any otherwise exposed emotional or mental damage. It's almost impossibly hard to go from being "Hey, I thought you were married", to "Whoa, you got divorced?!". It is, in and of itself, an entirely new identity. One that is thrust upon us almost without notice, because we get so wrapped up in the distractions of taking care of our own, and especially our own "business" that relationships as well as being a sibling and a child to parents (if said parents are still in the earthly picture) can take the proverbial back-seat. Sure, we can even attempt to shoulder our share of the blame as if this whole thing was our idea, especially if it helps us heal faster. This is not always the case, but kudos to those who could make that work.

I recall practicing that tactic several times. It works when I needed it to, but at the end of the day, it takes some honest-to-goodness purging and "personal identification" recovery, persistence, excruciating patience, and finally, the motivation to get started reinventing ourselves and rediscovering our life. Otherwise this self-imposed and self-inflicted cross we give ourselves may aid to give us the illusion that we are someone we wish we weren't. Why I refer to that as an illusion is because it isn't who we really are. It's not easy, and it's quite painful, both emotionally and even mentally. However, there is a sincere and critical need to embrace our new identity and run with it (walk first, then lightly jog, gaining your proverbial confidence, then take off running). There's no use in getting angry or upset with our circumstances over that reality. Barring any unusual circumstances in a traditional family setting and relationship, we need, for the most part, experience, as we are with our spouse nearly every single day. So how did we *not* see this cataclysmic event coming? There are those who will argue that no one could have seen it coming. For us well intended spouses, we would like to think that we saw everything coming and we knew our spouse well enough that we knew when there was something amiss. Especially when there IS something missing. That once obvious light has now dimmed, and trickled into the total darkness.

Divorces aren't really about what we missed, per se, but more about, *why* we missed it. Whatever "it" is in any given relationship. It's terrifying to think that we are losing our spouse, our marriage, our happiness, because we missed that one thing. That one intangible 'variable" that we thought was the source of our happiness and that "it" would give us a true sense of self and comprehensively, our intrinsic meaning. In a sense, losing who we are. I don't know about the rest of you, but when I faced that daunting prospect, my first thoughts immediately turned to the long, painstaking, and at least initially, un-motivation to want to start all over. The rebuilding of so many things that made me who I was. I was terrified of what I was going to do *then*. Admittedly, it was a very emotional knee-jerk response to what presented as seemingly negative stimuli. If we were all able to somehow go *from* being "emotional" with our decision-making to a more rational, analytical decision-making mind-set, we can quickly have a better understanding of ourselves and embrace this new life ahead of! Because - believe it or not (and I cannot say this with enough emphasis) not only is there LIFE after divorce, but most importantly, it's BETTER than we ever could dream of!!

Here's one of the best secrets I can tell you about post-divorce trauma: you're not going to make yourself happy by shutting out your pain. Because even when you *look* happy on the outside, everyone else is going to assume the pain is gone, which can be just another clever façade. So, now that we convince ourselves we are ready to be divorced, how do we go about *acting* divorced? Do we continue to act guilty or loveless? Some argue that 0ne can't feel that much guilt without having loved to that degree. Some will assume that we had love and let it go as if it was nothing more than a silly helium balloon. Who really cares, anyway? We divorcee's all know the real inner truth, don't we? Act happy on the outside yet, suffering on the inside,. Thus giving the notion that the length of our marriage and the experiences we endured really all meant nothing. Right? So very wrong!

Ignoring the pain just causes it to be buried deeper and deeper like a bad seed strategically planted in our hearts like then-ingenious Trojan Horse. Pain, if not dealt with, embraced, and processed, will destroy us. Its diabolical nature is to be grafted in and slither around until it is deeply rooted in the worst places inside, and then, it *strikes* with such stealth with the intent to render its captive useless and unable to fight back.

Pain leads to discomfort mentally, emotionally, and spiritually. Which may lead to any number of symptoms ranging from resentment, anger, a distorted and negative perspective all desensitizing the emotions with only one goal and one destination in its path. Just like the Trojan Horse, pain wants complete destruction and disassembling of the human soul. Check yourself frequently. If pain really does play a part in your mood, attitude and your associations with others - *deal with it*! Throw rocks in a nearby lake, vent to a friend, seek therapy. Get It OUT!! Happy persons can identify a pain-induced victim ten times out of ten. Some may choose to want to help; others will reject the pain-filled person and want no further involvements with that for fear of infection. Pain is as real as any epidemic that ever has been, or ever will be. Pain is cousin to misery, and we all know that misery loves company. Pain will leave us tormented about who we are. Ache over our circumstances, writhe over our perceived "broken family". And if it could get worse, pain and misery will corrupt our foreseeable future.

Shifting gears, I, the author of this book, am sorry for your circumstances and situations. I am sorry you are going through this. I am equally sorry that whoever loved you (or claimed to love you) placed you firmly in the "Divorced" column (If you are divorced). It's not all your fault. It's not. You, the reader are *not* unlovable and you are *not* unworthy to be in a relationship, or even *not* deserving to be in a relationship. Those people in your lives made their choices. Just like we make our choices. We all will be held accountable for our decision making. Again, I'm sorry any of us must go through these trials. On the upside, any pain we suffer, any heartbreak, any discomforts, frustration, and disassociation we experience, the Lord will always be there to bless us and compensate for any weaknesses and any soul sucking voids we are so desperately entrenched. He is there for us in this most excruciating time of need. Because (and trust me on this) living in misery sucks marginally less than dying in it. We just need to remember to turn to Him. As I've said countless times before, "His hand is stretched out still". Just like the adversary has fabricated and counterfeited everything, so that everything has its opposite, on the opposite side of *that* coin, is God's original version of everything He's created.

Purity, virtue, kindness, patience, charity, and love; the list goes on forever. They are the things that are "as they are supposed to be." All we need to do is knock.

Never resent "Love" over your divorce. Love didn't hurt you. Someone that didn't know *how* to love, hurt you.

When Children Are Involved

If you are a parent of younger children, sometimes you have inner dialogues with yourself to try to imagine what they might, or would say to you - or about you, if you could do more than just *hear* them; but really *listen* to what they say. If we focus on that thought, what do we think our children would they say if they said the worst possible things about us? Would they call us out on all our perceived thoughts? Could you *hear* what they are honestly trying to say? Could we understand from more than a parent's perspective if our child were to look us square in the eye and ask us "Where were you on the night of my recital? Why did you have to work?" Most, if not all young children need to know that their parents love them, and that both parents care. It's an intrinsic trait inside most, if not all children need from their earliest developmental stages, to adolescence and beyond. Granted the degree of want of acceptance and love from outside sources of parents, siblings and others ebbs and flows. But overall, it's a basic instinct, a very primal need. We as parents have a divine responsibility to harvest, nurture, encourage, and develop those essential feelings of love, want and acceptance towards our children. Because they know, every night when we leaned over and kissed them on the forehead or on the cheek; when we give them a big warm hug and exemplify and reinforce that we do love them and we do care. Their comprehension, and situational awareness kicks in. Then comes that moment of gravity: it's as if we see them growing up right before our eyes, right then and there! When they say those things that not only tear at your heartstrings, but darn near sever them. Then they begin to state their case. For instance, confronting us about some of our adult misdeeds, like not being there for them exactly when they needed us to be. Despite us telling them all throughout their growing up, telling them repeatedly that we would be there for them. What message does that send to our children? If that has ever been the case with us as parents, (and it likely is on hopefully less frequent occasions) how can our kids continue to take us seriously? I'm no child psychologist, or therapist, but I wouldn't be surprised if that might be one of many reasons why children act out. Perhaps somewhere in our "raising" them, we've somehow let them down (do keep in mind that *their* perception *is* their reality) and parenting is a nearly impossible task to never let your kids down. When it comes to parenting, following your heart is simple, as if it's always easier to react emotionally when it comes to those little carbon-based copies of us (children). Following your brain is the difficult part, as it basically removes any emotion, and makes your next move(s) more calculated, more mechanical, leaving room for our logical side to think and rethink (almost ad nauseam) all the potential outcomes of a situation as it pertains to our children. Especially after so long of heeding the "advice" of our heart. Ergo why all parents most likely end up failing children at various points in their upbringing. It happens. Any parent who thinks they can honestly say that they have never failed or disappointed their children is in denial. It happens, and it will continue to be the case in the foreseeable parental future. Don't misunderstand; this action isn't the worst thing that can happen. I'm not sharing this perspective as any kind of "downer", but more of a way to address a trending issue. For centuries this has plagued parent-kind, so we can properly broach it and embrace it, rather than deny it. Embracing the issue is cousin to certitude. It allows for reparations and acceptance and improvement. Denial, like every other pejorative adjective, is a tool and a device of the adversary. It is intended (in this case and example) to pollute and distort the reality that improvement and overcoming those less than ideal circumstances with parenting and children's behaviors is not only very possible, but a virtual, and eternal certainty!

Embrace the trials ahead with our kids. Embrace trials as if they were our own children and *love them!* Solace and peace are the pending byproduct! I promise. Because I've seen in my own life, as well as witnessed it in my fellow divorced friends lives and in other's lives. Trials will come. They will always be there, waiting to test us and our fortitude. It's the blessings thereafter that make the rocky, and inconvenient trail worth the trek. Put our heads down and do the work.

I would never presume to give absolute advice or "best practice" suggestions to parents in pending "separated from spouse" and/or divorce circumstances. Or how to address the topic with your kids of "how we're moving forward as a family" without knowing some very specific details first. With that said, I'll address some more frequent and popular circumstances that I do have sound experience in, as this is a very difficult and controversial issue in most, if not all families, that suffer this unfortunate, but also fortunate circumstance.

I say "fortunate" because not all divorces are necessarily bad. Sure, the circumstances which brought about the divorce can be unfortunate, but the end of a divorce can also mean a change for the better - the *infinitely* better. Spouses and children who find themselves in an emotionally and even (heaven forbid) a physically abusive relationship and/or family environment, DO NOT need or deserve to remain in that destructive environment. The sad element and disposition here, is that many spouses and children stay in this unnecessary situation and circumstance for the wrong reason(s). "Sticking it out" (meaning remaining in the abusive relationship) "for the sake of the kids" is no longer (and in my personal opinion, never was) a good enough excuse! Any spouse, husband, father, wife, mother that engages in any form of abusive behavior who refuses to acknowledge that there is, in fact a problem, or refuses to seek the much-needed help and counselling, shouldn't be considered "co-habitable". There's just no rhyme, reason, excuse, or disposition that can, or will ever justify their abuse. Persons that pursue a divorce in these abusive circumstances ought to consider these three actions:

1) Inform their immediate family: parents and siblings and any associates of the abuse and seek help, relief and support.
2) Always seek for the protection, and support towards the children. They need to know it's not their fault, nor is it anything they've done to deserve the treatment in this situation.
3) Seek counsel from a qualified professional. And if you have access to your local bishopric or other ecclesiastical leadership, inform them of the situation as well.

These three actions are not easy at all. If they are easy, then good for you! You might just be ahead of the curve, or you've reached your breaking point and are ready to execute an effective course of action to further protect your family before it's too late. If they do seem difficult, or even impossible, consider the alternative: you and your children can and will continue to be exposed to the forms of abuse your spouse is perpetrating. Perspective is reality, it *truly* is. Don't be afraid to act! Some of the best outcomes in history, both documented and undocumented came from those who were afraid, cripplingly so, to execute a course of action, but somehow found the strength and fortitude and take action, despite their inner terror. Even despite the odds and despite the impossible uncertainty of the future that lies ahead. By the way, that "somehow" comes from a Divine Heavenly Parent that is doing what you as a parent, are also doing, and looking out for their beloved children.

Reset

Life has a funny way of messing us up and keeping us on our toes. Or what seems like pulling the proverbial rug out from underneath us. Before the rug is pulled, It's as if we can totally see it coming, but for a split-second, we are in a temporary, momentary stage of denial. Like it's being viewed in a 3rd-person, slow-motion screenplay. We're hoping to everything that when we see the camera angle, (if you will) that the primary perspective of the person that the said events are happening to. That the angle/perspective reflects the angle of some "extra" or "co-star". Then the gravity of our situation hits like a sinister plot-twist.

When the imaginary camera panned and subsequently zoomed in on me, as the "star" of this emotional horror film, my heart sank. I flat out wasn't ready. Not by a longshot. I felt like I was the Quarterback getting sacked on my blindsided by a three-hundred and fifty-pound defensive lineman. My body damage was minimal however, my emotional and mental damage was catastrophic.

After the damage had set in, what I didn't expect to happen next, happened. This realization occurred to me, with me no longer having a wife in my life. No longer (for the time being) having my immediate family readily around me to bear me up and support me and no one to really turn to who had any clue at all what I was going through, it occurred to me that this was my chance to start over. This was a very rare and very unique opportunity. I get to hit the proverbial "reset" button on my life. There are a select few major choices that I was faced with in this all-too critical juncture. They didn't come to me all at once. It's as if they were all lined up, almost strategically, for me. With me being so very leery of my actual decision-making abilities and not wanting to deal with the consequential results, inasmuch as my decisions had led me to the Divorced Universe. I was of course, terrified if my decisions were to go awry. The question then became, was I going to use this moment, this opportunity to "reset" - as it were - at this check point? Could I choose correctly and have an opportunity for self-improvement? Or would I choose poorly, allowing my labeling circumstances to drag me down even further, encouraging and even condoning my own self-loathing, leading to my own self-defeat? As gripping as that reality might just be, I should have already known the answer to that. Admitting defeat is borderline masochistic (obviously, situations are very subjective and very much case-by-case) with few and limited redeeming merits, albeit self-contrived. Admitting defeat is quite the pejorative mentality. I prefer to acknowledge this situation as sacrificing an irreparable marriage for the sake of my moral code and religious standards. I knew that God should win every time. Which is why (and I'll continue to address this over and over in this book) staying and remaining in bad relationships, sacrificing one's own happiness for the sake of a failing marriage, and/or for the sake of one's children is not only enabling and facilitating the poor treatment of ones opposing spouse, but also is no longer a valid reason to remain in bad relationships. For, in so doing, we are in one degree showing our children that poor behavior and treatment of another's spouse is not only to be tolerated, but is acceptable. It can, in most cases, pass on the example to our children other very bad relationships, habits and behaviors.

The Lord didn't want me to be so unhappy in my condemned relationship. This cesspool of a marriage not only took away from me who I was as a man, (which it did, albeit temporarily) but also took away my happiness and jeopardized and even threatened my religious standards and aspirations. Even more importantly, had the dire potential to take away everything I've lived for, and everything I'd served for. My failed marriage threatened everything I've ever held near and dear, and spilled the same blood, in the same emotional mud (so to speak). Deep down inside, I knew it was wrong. So, I learned to let my past go, with all the toxic and residual sand and rust of many murky memories in my emotional and mental wake. I don't ever look back, because I'm not headed in that direction.

When I faced that imperative and inevitable juncture, I realized I possessed the agency to be very, very creative. I decided I'd take a "whack" at this new concept called "decision-making" and then execute my decisions as a direct result! I was kind of terrified at first, I won't lie. But I found some things out about myself. Firstly, that I was, what I refer to as a "thinker". What I mean by that is, I had the ability to not only think things through, but thoroughly and effectively. I could almost "see" any and every potential outcome of a situation. Even better, I was now able to successfully predict and or see the outcomes of various situations the majority of times! Now, I'm not suggesting that I am at all any sort of clairvoyant per se, but rather a basic, yet diligent plotter, planner, and schemer. I LOVE to plan, anticipate, explore, conceive, and execute a game plan.

What made this so great for me in my own self-rediscovery was that it was also subsequently rebuilding my confidence! It was a strangely awakening feeling, nascent, gaining emotional momentum, building confidence, and piecing me and my sanity back together. I never really lost my sanity per se (I realize that according to some, that may be debatable) but I did feel that my sanity, with this particular example and metaphor I'm about to create, was like a jigsaw puzzle. At various points through my divorce, these pieces were being stretched apart. It's crazy to me now, how these pieces never snapped off. Despite my willingness to just let go of any piece, not caring what piece of my sanity fell away, only if it provided some sort of release. Or maybe, in spite of it. I would try most anything, if it meant I would sleep better at night (At this point, I was only getting about 3-4 hours of sleep per night because of the perpetual, incessant stress.), or somehow prevent me from waking up to a tear-soaked pillow that I had finally fallen asleep on. Only because my over-active brain is still grinding out thoughts and hypothetical situations so daunting, that I would start to believe the worst possible scenarios that I've conceived. Albeit only in my mind. And the body just can't keep up with the mind anymore. I would stay wide awake, praying to anything or anyone that would listen to my incessant cries for relief, until ultimate and total exhaustion set in. My body gave into the pending unconsciousness. However, for only a brief few hours before my body has recharged, just enough to snap back awake. It seemed as though my body would be so overtaken by stress, that it would recharge (sleep) only long enough to jolt itself back up again! Only now, my hyperactive brain activity could commence holding my sanity and overall functionality hostage with no clue as to what unremitting ransom my brain might require.

For me, it was different every day. It affected my work, which my employer at the time, and the management could not be more unsympathetic. This added more negative stress on me, as the risk of losing my job in the middle of a divorce is catastrophic for one's self-esteem. As if matters could not be any worse! Then again, they only got to see me and my tough exterior, they didn't get the opportunity to know what was purging in my delicate male psyche. The emotional distortion effected my socializing, my family life, my relationship with my children (although they provided some much-needed release and relief as well) and even worse, my relationship with my immediate family. This ebbed and flowed every single night and morning. If anything can be said about my darkest hours (more like my darkest months) it's that it was consistently *inconsistent*. This is also equally, if not more infuriating. I found myself wanting to just fade away. I wanted to disappear both body and soul. I was never truly suicidal. Taking my life was never an option. My children are everything and more, and worth living through anything for. When I broke down and really got to the heart of the matter, I didn't want to 'feel' anything anymore, to the point that I was desensitizing myself. It was the only release that was generating results. So, like any other consumer, I fed that cause in what I hoped was to dull the pain. Dulling the pain has its inherent risks, however. I've seen many friends try to desensitize themselves to the point of garnering (temporary) psychological disorders. Sometimes they may not even recognize it. These (temporary) desensitizing techniques are more subtle than a cold or a physical injury. There are those that a believe that the adversary thrives in this realm. He loves to hide out in the more secret, often neglected corners of our minds and souls and when the moment is right, he strikes. It is not so much a guerrilla-type tactic, but slow, easy, and seemingly painless. He's calculated and precise. He's merciless and mercilessly persistent. However, despite all his strengths, he's conquerable. He's very beatable. He has his limitations. His biggest limitation is our agency. He cannot dictate how and what we choose unless we use our God-given agency to do so. By heeding and acting on his various temptations, he can, however strongly influence what we do, and tempt us to the point of breaking our willpower, if we use our agency to let him. This kind of giving control to the adversary terrifies me. He's only as powerful as we give him of our power. He's the "give me an inch and I'll take eternity" type villain. He will want to desensitize the souls of men and women to not only doing something spiritually stupid, but to *keep* doing those stupid things that will draw us farther and farther away from our Heavenly Home. Something that I've tried to remain very self-conscious of is not to desensitize myself into a sociopath, psychopath, or a narcissist. Being accountable and responsible are big in my book (both literally in this book, and in my metaphorical personal 'book'). So, checking myself to see if I still feel empathy, and sincerity and not just a practiced apathy is critical for me. I'm not any kind of expert, nor will I ever confess to be. I will say, however that my experiences in life and divorce and love are all excruciating task-masters. They have provided me with experiences and life lessons that are invaluable to me! My spiritual side and my mental side usually play very well together. When

I feel the Spirit and when my mental facilities communicate that experience to me, that's been a solidifying experience to me that what I feel and what I experience, and now what I know is true and comes from God. It's been my experience that when those elements are effectively communicated, holding to the word of God, and sometimes even "alternating/adjusting my grip" on His words, to get a better view of my surroundings, gives me the assurance and the perspective that the world isn't the answer, nor does it have the answers to its own problems.

Becoming Something

We all have those tender personal moments. Those moments where we close our eyes and even just for a split second, we're able to stop time. For the moment, escape our current reality, and somehow and think back to a memory. A memory that, at the time, made us happy. Maybe it was a moment where we truly believe that everyone important in our lives loved us unconditionally. That notion alone would do it for us. Meaning that this thought could release us from any feelings of depression, rejection, or any sensations of personal inadequacy. Just that single moment of clarity, where we were somehow able to block out the noise of our troubles, stress, newfound singlehood, shield off the outside world if even but for a moment, and just focus on what our heart wants to say. I think we would be surprised. I think we would be surprised at the stories that our heart would tell our mind, if our mind could receive it. It's times like this that I found myself being discouraged about being so human, and considering the impact of my mortality on my being. What was so discouraging for a logical and analytical guy like me, was trying to somehow logically and emotionally connect one's own heart and mind so that they too are somehow on the same page. Every time I would try to synchronize my heart and my mind, (an odd practice, I know) I usually end up either out-thinking and then, even over-thinking my emotions. Which then resulted in to *how* I reacted to my emotions. Sometimes, while I am scanning my consciousness, wanting results even to the extent of imagining my emotions to somehow communicate anything to myself. I believe that this sort of introspection, that ability to take stock of one's life, is far more important than we realize. I was in such a metaphysical state once, that my heart and mind didn't connect at all. I considered the meaning of truth, how earth and heaven above played any part in this conundrum. How emotions are basically the only thing that we had to focus on to make sense of all the destructive thoughts running amok in our mind. Or, maybe we are just afraid that if we were to consider another version *of* the truth that we might find out that we are a good person that just made bad choices! Or that somehow, perhaps our actions leading up to a certain decision being made might possibly make us a bad person. I don't feel that way about that kind of the scenario, personally. I think that good people can do bad things. I think that good people make bad choices. I likewise believe that the same said "good people" learn and learn quickly from said bad things.

Let's examine *"truth"* and what should be understood about it as it pertains to becoming something before, during, and especially after one's divorce.

What elements do we need to have familiarity with to possess the reality of our story? It's often been said that there's always three sides to every story: In the case and situation of divorce and breakups, there's the primary side of the story which belongs to us. Then there's the other spouse/partner's version of the story (usually construed to the bias of their perspective). Then finally, there's the (usually) more truthful version, which is most often "somewhere in between". Or maybe the truth is what we need to finish our own version of the tale. Either way, the truth will always have its day. I have found that this is a matter of me coming to grips with the reality that the truth is the truth, and always will be the truth. I realize how redundant that sounds, but hear me out: Truth is eternal and unchanging. Two plus two will always equal four, and humans and mortals will always breathe oxygen. Lies, and/or untruths are imperfect, limited and have an expiration date. The key, I found, is that I need to *execute with the intent to succeed*. In the same breath, I can't be afraid to fail either. Failure really isn't as bad as the negative connotation that perpetually trails it. Failure is just the next step to success. It's just discovering one or several ways in which our objective isn't achieved. There's always several ways to accomplish something. Now, what to become, you may ask? May I counter with: What do we want to be? What is it in your current situation that has you wanting to do better or be better or want more? Or a combination of all three? Where do we want to go? What do we want to achieve? It's not just any stage in life that anyone gets the legitimate opportunity to re-shape and re-mold one's life all over again. It's a sacred, yet daunting task. It needs to be calculated. It requires sincere thought, execution, and endurance. Because nothing - and no one great - ever comes easy. I have worked and strived and fought battles unseen and otherwise unnoticed, that most any and everyone else would have happily surrendered to and runaway from. I've made so many mistakes and so many people have paid a certain price on unspeakable emotional platforms because of my poor choice of words, timing, positioning and even actions. For some time, I pled ignorance and just didn't know any better. I endured it and squared my shoulders and plowed through wall after wall. I plowed through brick after brick, until the only thing left standing was me. I "looked back" metaphorically and I panned the surface to see if there were any other challengers, and there were. They just existed on the next "level up". Then came the challenge of "stepping up". It's the natural process of things. Progress or parish, as some would say. Becoming something implies so many different metaphors. I'll focus my efforts on the ones at hand, as in "leveling up". It's not a simple task; it's daunting and lengthy. It's rough and forces the best out of us. I won't give up on it or myself, especially not the same way I've *been* given up on by those around me throughout my life. That experience isn't intended to provoke any sympathy or empathy for me. I don't want it, nor need it. I'm not a victim. I am, however, a direct result of my tears, trials and consequential triumphs. There's more hope and divine strength than I've ever realized. Better yet, it's "low-hanging fruit".

One of the reasons why it's metaphorically called "fruit" is that it's "out on a limb". We have to be bold, take a chance, change and stretch ourselves against our norms and redefine our boundaries.

There are those, few and far between, but are a growing populous that are finding something out about themselves. They are finding what can be referred to as the "Creator within". This is something, believe it or not, that we *all* have within us. Trials abound in this life. Even the rich, and the famous, and the most spiritual persons endure trials. They come in all varies. Too many to number, and too many examples to give credence to any select few. What many are finding out about themselves, (and I hope and pray that all of us do, especially those reading this book) realize, recognize and then exemplify, is the ability to turn everything into something good. This doesn't come easy. There is a certain level of mental and emotional discipline. Some real earthly, as well as eternal perspective. This characteristic is indicative of our divine lineage. It is, in so many words, a godly characteristic. Our Heavenly Father always seems able to do this. Everything, no matter how dire, becomes a victory to the Lord. Joseph who was sold into Egypt, although a slave and wholly undeserving of this fate, nevertheless remained faithful to the Lord and continued to live the commandments and made something very good of his degrading circumstances. People like this cannot be defeated. Now, am I implying that all of us share Joseph's destiny? No, Not hardly. I am implying that there are those of us that discover this divine trait inside of us. Once we do, we start creating. Creating businesses, that bless the lives of others as well as our own. Creating blogs, for connecting persons of interest to help support and aide one another. Special interest groups that bond and connect communities and social groups that otherwise would never meet their potential, and even worse, their inherent design and goals.

Don't be limited by your mortal eyesight. Learn to see what's visible beyond the eye. Develop your eternal perspective, and learn to see the world through your Heavenly Father's eyes. He created the world out of essentially missing pieces. He can help us with our "Creatorship" Then with His help and his guidance, we too, will become undefeatable.

On the Emotional Mend

When I've endured those quiet moments of reflection, self-pity, soul-searching, self-empathy, rationalization, justification, and ultimately soul-defining character, I'm in total control. I get to choose. My choice is this: I can either point my proverbial finger at others, my circumstances, my situation(s), my employment, my familial support (or seemingly, the lack thereof) friends, (the list of scapegoats is nearly endless). Or, I can choose to be filled with resolve and grab on to that Iron Rod I've taught about in the scriptures all these years. The choice is mine. We are all free to choose. It's given to us as a divine gift. It's a travesty that we don't treat our agency as it is so divinely instituted. The late Elder Neal A. Maxwell said it best: "Yes! We mortals are still free to choose! Yes! A war was even fought in heaven to preserve our moral agency. Yet down here, the divine gift of agency is often surrendered without so much as a mild whimper."

(October 2001 General Conference, "The Seventh Commandment, A Shield").

Here, in this delicate time of trial, limbo, and inner natural disaster, I came to come to know a large part of who I really was. Fear can be a distracting factor, as its intent is to lead us away from confidence and peace. These two traits are ever so vital in our pursuit of the real "us". Fear, at least initially, lead me to a path that I could see and a sense of that appealed to my natural man tendencies. It was the coward in me that falls into the Dark Princes enticings and his path-of-least-resistance soul-numbing, desensitizing solicitations. The path of that leads to the rationalization and justification away any remaining spiritual sensitivity in exchange for physical sensory gratification. The junction, as it were, was to go the way of indulging my senses, repeatedly. Of the which, I saw in some of my friends and occasionally in myself, that causes the realization that with every indulgence gratified, draws the "taste buds" of my soul not only to a sense for the want for more indulging, but dulls and deadens my soul and spirit. The pursuit of such is not only never ending, but also desensitizing to the point where "Of whom a man is overcome, of the same he is brought into bondage". These indulgences are not only designed to numb our senses, but can and will, if we let them, drain any remaining sense of inner-self, and self-respect, and consequently, self-regard. Lust, desires and passions can consume any remaining soul-vacancies, whereby drawing us further into self-consumption, and consequently, further and further away from the out-stretched hand of He who loves us unconditionally, and desires to give us, his children, all that He has.

Again, it's our choice. We can either choose the most priceless independence of being free from the unforgiving, soul-damaging bondage of sin. To slowly, yet enticingly dancing away to the beat coming from the crowd surrounding and worshipping the "Golden Calf", as they dance and rave in the foundationless direction of the Great and Spacious Building. Consider the alternative: the redeeming and soul-satisfying light that comes from our Heavenly Father. This same light will constantly shine clarion through any darkness and all untruths. We are all allowed to use our agency to act, and spiritually maneuver within the protection, and inspiration of a Holy Heavenly Father, who's only desire is to bring us home in His safety. Both have eternal consequences and ramifications. Then, there's the moment that I never really saw coming. The moment that I was some-crazy-how wanting to transpire. The moment that I saw, felt, and somehow conceptualized, everything I've ever understood, based any personal beliefs (founded or not) isn't that it was costumed, or "made-up" to be. It's the moment that, not just myself, or fate, or happenstance has been waiting for. But it's the moment that *truth* had been waiting for. On many and levels of our lives, we may try to hide from, elude, escape, and/or cheat the truth. But like all eternal things, the truth will endure any amount of questioning, falsehoods, depravity, skepticism, contradictions, and any attempt to out-smart the truth. Someday, (and mark my words) all ill-conceived attempts to falsify, malign, twist, alter, offset, and shift the truth will disappear like the author they originated from (Lucifer). At some point, the truth will have its day. What is most important, (and it cannot be overstated) is what side of the truth's "coming up" party are we going to be standing on? If we are on the Lords side, who or what could possibly be against us?

Unrealized Power within Us

Doesn't it seem like sometimes that what once was a historical declaration of pending peril in the phrase: "Rome is Burning" seems to hit more closely to home in our personal, subconscious, intuitive and interpersonal lives? Even though that declaration can have many meanings for a garden-variety of perilous situations, I still somehow perpetually found myself elbows-deep in a cesspool of toxic emotions. As I scrambled about, trying to figure out the "emotional arithmetic" as it were, but here lies the problem: I didn't have all the numbers. The formula to the equation is incomplete. The question then becomes, how *do* we find the answers? What is the "order of operations" to find the missing variables? Or there are some of us that just give up entirely. Left alone, we may feel, and choose to alienate or even isolate themselves, while they slowly sink into the stagnant swamp of self-pity.

Rise above. Our divine nature within us stirs at the prospect of being initialized. As if further pondering and introspection unlocks the "keycode". I declare the term "keycode" to explain two different concepts rolled into one word. "Key" to indicate the mechanism, or tool, as it were, to "unlock" an otherwise inanimate object. "Code" as to suggest that the data/intel is "password protected" and special clearance or that currently is has a secret meaning.

So, we progress to the point where we dig deep in our minds, perhaps a dialogue similar to this line of questioning: "What is a *true* disciple? Why should I be diligent? Why should I discipline my passions, habits and "Natural Man" tendencies? What's next after victory?" It's no surprise that for most, if not all of us have asked these types of questions since we were young. For some of us, it's the basis of our belief system. At some point, we had to decide, either to forget about those questions, or to further the fight to find the "keycode" to who we divinely *really are.* I got discouraged with this path, or approach, as the adversary absolutely does not want me to discover my celestial identity! Because, in this mortal life, I will eventually come to find out how far away I really am to my true divinity. As long as we have firm opposition and fierce trials to challenge and promote our growth, I will keep fighting! The purpose of all our trials is to understand one of the gospel's primary objectives behind my trials and troubles. The gospel of Jesus Christ creates spiritual warriors, and Divine Nobility. Not cowards and rebels.

Monotonous Relatonships

So, you're in a relationship. Things become shall we say, "predictable" or maybe even repetitive. For instance, the once charming, funny man has become repetitive, nay borderline mechanical. He doesn't bring treats, or surprises, or flowers as often, if any more. Guys, she's gone from "whispering sweet nothings" in your ear to breathing out threatening's if her "honey-do" list isn't getting the attention she thinks it deserves. Try as we might, these nights and days do, and ultimately *will* happen. So now what? Take another failed attempt to "spice things up" or even just more cleverly "mix" things up? Perhaps, but it seems like the last attempt lingered for a while, but after some time, things kind of digressed back to the original. Instead of watching your shared favorite TV series together, all curled up on the couch under a blanket that was once charming and endearing, is now a recipe for nostalgic reverberations of "golly, gee, remember when…?" and we reminisce over what *used* to be. We look at each other as if to say, even simultaneously: "What happened to us?" Only to quickly look away, and go back to acting as if we're both safely tucked away in the most precious of "honeymoon stages" semi-happy married people try to convince themselves that they are in love– daily. It may never solve what is wrong in the first place.

Could love songs be right? Is love enough, or isn't it? I suppose it is contingent on how one defines love, or even love-like actions. Is it the "little things" as all the hopeless romantics may believe? Is it the frequency of being served and taken care of by your spouse? Or, is it what you want to and choose to do for them, to demonstrate this so called "love"? There's so much more to that eternal emotion and trait than we mere mortals can ever expect to comprehend in this fallen sphere. We must go to the source, the source of all love. We must know what role we play and how to embrace it. It's not easy.

I struggle with a certain apology, and how it may or may not be received, if at all.

It isn't the apology that will mend long years of suffering or long years of confusion and emotional distortion. It isn't even the apology of how maybe two could have tried a little harder for and with each other. It's the apology that deep down inside that I know I'll never get. The apology that my children will never get. That apology - my bent-not-broken family will never get. That's the secret to getting by, isn't it? Prematurely accepting the apology you'll never get. Accepting the fact that despite whatever 'wrongs' were thrown at you, and each time your mind plays them back for you, they intensify. They grow, nearly taking on personalities and lives of their own. And with one fatal blow they can own you and your other thoughts, commanding attention whenever they want some mental 'bandwidth' from you.

It's that time again to put "pen to paper" (or, fingertips on keys, in this case as it were) and bleed on the page. If there is one thing I truly do love about writing, is the rare and limited ability to articulate feelings. Beginning with how my mind creates scenarios and how my nervous system experiences them and somehow connect how they feel, into a more tangible, less abstract sequence of syntax in the form of words on a page. I'm going to start this chapter off with a phrase I fell in love with while talking to a friend about advanced relationships. It was on those conversations where it started off as any other; casual, innocent, well-intentioned and, as any other conversation can mature and progress, it's something more deeply profound than initially intended. They said: "we all want the relationship we currently don't have."

Relationships in a more adult setting are very trying because of their complexities, multiple factors and facets, advanced thinking of both more jaded, as well as more experienced participants. Oft times we find ourselves only hanging on by a very thin thread because it's the only way we know how to "hold on". Although there are many factors, the one that I find most prevalent - and this may be just for me, but it's also because one of the worst practices and habits is to try and find meaning in an otherwise meaningless relationship. So many of us try so hard to hope against hope, in an effort to find what it is we have been looking for all along. I have these inner emotional conversations about how I feel about myself. How you may dislike yourself and even hate yourself, albeit for the time being. How you feel and how you even feel about how you feel, which may sound redundant. But it makes sense, trust me. You will not always like it, in fact you rarely will get used to it. The course we take, will take some time - some desensitization of your own emotions, even to the point of dehumanization. It ebbs and flows. Here and there we experience it all over again as if renewed afresh. It's the enduring that causes so much pain.

The temptation I found during this process is that it's easy to want to rethink all the pain I suffered, all the heartache, and the emotional hurricane's that I endured, somehow. I'll reflect on those experiences again and again. I'll wear the trauma in my mind and heart like a badge of honor. Like a true badge of honor, as if imagining the emotional war that was waged on me and my relationship and in my head the images are still vivid, alive and well.

I would never presume that going through my divorce is anything close to the unmatched pain suffering and starvation that the early Christian Pioneers had to endure. I only have their experiences as their written accounts to try and somehow relate to. As if comparing my pain and heartache and disappointment could ever *be* measured or compared to theirs. If I were honest with myself, I'd say that there is absolutely no comparison. It's essentially comparing apples to oranges. What even brought about this comparison in the first place goes back to my statement about the vivacity of the images and how lifelike they still remain in my mind. John Breen, a 15-year old Christian Pioneer made this profound statement when the Pioneers finally reached their destination:

"It was long after dark when we got to Johnson's Ranch, so the first time I saw it was early in the morning. The weather was fine, the ground was covered with green grass, the birds were singing from the tops of the trees, and the journey was over. I could scarcely believe that I was alive.

"The scene that I saw that morning seems to be photographed on my mind. Most of the incidents are gone from memory, but I can always see the camp near Johnson's Ranch." This next statement may seem incredibly unlikely for some onlookers who, like us that have no clue what the pioneers suffered, to imagine how all the pains a divorcee has suffered, only to acknowledge that some, if not most of the worse of "our incidents" are "gone from memory". How can that be? D. Todd Christofferson shared his crystal-clear explanation in his insights. He states that it is a form of forgiveness, as a gift from our Heavenly Father. So why do some perhaps otherwise horrific images remain in our head? I personally believe so that we can remember from where, and what we've come. A lot, if not most of the memorable pain may be taken away, but memories remain to help us where we have come from and where we're going. These pains can and should expand our gratitude. Perhaps most importantly, the blessing and the Divine Parenting the Lord has given us in the form of a better future.

So how do we escape the lethargic grasps of relationship monotony? There are so many ways! Husbands, fiancé`s, and boyfriends, think to yourself, (and think hard) what is/was it about your wife that spun your head around the first, second and third (plus) times? What separated her from *all* of the other ladies? Why *her*? Honestly, if you have to ask more questions beyond that, you may want to ask yourself if you really love her. However, the point is, *fall in love with her all over again!* Yes! Find ways and reasons to love her, but more than just that! Look at her, the way she moves in her favorite dress, or a dress that you got her. The hypnotic sound of her heels on the hard wood floor (or any hard surface) and close your eyes, and envision – *her*. Before you ever saw her, and as those heels draw closer to you, you try to imagine exactly how beautiful she's going to look! Only to realize that was a fools errand, because no matter how imaginative we are, she will always look 1,000 times better when you see her, meet her eyes to yours, than what you could have imagined.

Now, ladies. Same applies to you. I get that we guys are and can be what I affectionately refer to as "BDA's" (Big, Dumb, Animals) but we love you to death. Head-to-toe, out of control, we hope you know! Please for the sake of your marriage and your sanity, find new ways to love us back! We don't know how to admit it, but we need your love, approval, acceptance, devotion, loyalty, trust, and emotions invested in us. No number of romance novels will love you back the way your man can! Think back, to the moment you first saw him. His broad shoulders, his uncombed hair, his hoodie and jeans outfit. Okay, his perfectly tailored suit, and those arms! Recall how it was, and how it *will be*- to be held, and to have him hold you for the first time, forever *that* way. You deserve to have your man protect you, provide for you, give you security, and peace, and a place you can call (and decorate to your hearts content) your home. Ladies, we need you. We need your validation, and assurance that we are *yours*. Guys, the same can and should *absolutely* be said of us! Reciprocity is key in any and all marriages! You cannot give that which you don't have! If you don't give your love to your lady, how is she supposed to give it back? No go get back to loving each other, before it's too late. Before the title of this book becomes your own memoir.

The Next Level of Dating

No matter how hard you tried, or how good you are, nor even how many times you failed, but still got up, dusted yourself off, and went at it again repeatedly, but were still not rewarded with that coveted outcome. It gets even more tricky. How many of us really know what we want? The answer is for the large majority of us - none of us know what we want. We only think we do. We don't have the full eternal perspective that the Lord does. Which is why faith in Heavenly Father is so important. Because He *does* have the eternal perspective on things. To add the silver lining to our trials, He wants our happiness and has already has designed our happiness, even despite the trials we are enduring.

The problem I found with running away from my trials is that eventually I run out of time and places to hide in failed attempts to escape them. Even worse, they relentlessly followed me. I didn't want to endure them. They can be painful, test my patience, expand my character, and finally, improve my overall well-being. Doesn't sound so bad after all, does it? Oftentimes, we find ourselves just wanting the "baby" without the proverbial "labor pains"! One would think. We should be, however, very encouraged that regardless of any dead-end we come to, the Lord will always be at the end of that road. Because He can always pave a way for us back to Him and his Kingdom.

Alone again. Seems daunting enough of a prospect, right? I mean, when you live the solitary life of a single parent, there's some things you just can't change. And others you wouldn't even if you *had to*. The singles world is not very merciful. It can be quite brutal. Worst of all, we can be quite savage to each other. In some, and perhaps even most cases when dating, us singles can have a circle of friends to lean on; it's a great support to all involved. It can also be a great detriment. For instance, think of highschool. Now think of the rumors that flooded the halls between classes and lunch hour. The backbiting, the gossiping (nearly synonymous), the deceit, the

Real-time Soap Operas! Comparisons and metaphors describing abound! It's as if we're all finally trying to get back at the big bully on the playground that took the proverbial ball away from us. Except this time, the pre-emanating fists and kicks that were once used on the playground, have now progressed to the cyber platform, namely social media. Only this time, the weapons are far more advanced, and can do nearly irreparable damage in an immeasurably short amount of time.

Consequently, we can now point our aggression in the misplaced direction of that same daunting "playground bully", and we attack offending persons as if they themselves are the very one who took our family away from us in the first place. It goes well beyond face-to-face fisticuffs. I've personally witnessed it transition to a cyber-enabled "arms race", to see who can do the most damage first, or at least in the shortest amount of time. It's total puerility at its finest. There are virtually too many social media and digital platforms that are currently available to both meet, date, and even start a relationship with and a bad reputation spreads faster than a wildfire in the savanna. I learned very quickly and early that women talk; and when they do, it's like a cyber Atomic bomb exploding, when it's about a less than perfect experience they had with a guy.

I'll say this frequently in this manuscript that "perception is reality". How women perceive a less than perfect experience with a guy in even a casual dating experience is usually totally different than how the guys can see it! Yet, somehow it all came from the same shared experience. It goes both ways, unfortunately. On the one hand of the singles scene, I've encountered that there truly is opposition in all things. In the right singles circles, both digital and other, you will not find a more strengthening and supportive "protect its own kind" type of people than the divorced and singles clans. We can be so tightly knit, and have some of the most tragic events happen to us, that we can empathize on so many levels with others emotional turmoil and struggles, that we unknowingly automatically develop a kinship; a brother and sisterhood of sorts. While the cliché stands that "misery loves company" so do single and divorced persons as we love our kind. Although "misery" may play a part in our bonding and fellowship, we are a very happy and energetic and enjoyable people! For the imaginative *most* part.

It used to be that whenever I met a fellow divorced person, I would immediately feel my emotions and sensors tune down to a much lower level. Now, hear me out, it wasn't *because* they were divorced or that I looked down on or discriminated against them, that's hypocritical and unsavory. Quite the contrary! I didn't really recognize it at first, but after so many instances, I started to pay closer attention. I realized I was taking on this perspective to be more understanding and empathetic to their situation. Looking back on it now, I realize that it is and was totally unnecessary and in a sense, a fool's errand. But I meant well, most of the time. I love these people. The divorcee's. We share a unique bond and are on common ground that is emblematic of a warzone; nigh even an emotional battlefield. Metaphorically, we've spilled the same blood, in the same mud. Fewer people can more closely relate. More persons can only imagine what those trenches are like. Sure, there's the proverbial emotional scars, but all scars are, all that they really showcase is that whatever tried to harm and/or kill us, failed. We became stronger as a result. A divorce will test you. It will show a person what they're *really* made of, and even expose you to your weakest traits, and your greatest strengths. While we will casually graze over our strengths, we will obsess at times over our weaknesses. This absolutely shows up in dating. I feel women have (to a certain favorable extent) an advantage in this area because they are already emotionally-based creatures, so they deal with their emotions on a regular basis. I'm inclined to believe that as a direct result of the fairer sex being far more familiar with their emotions by comparison to us guys, so they know more aptly what their emotions mean to them. It's one of the many reasons why us guys don't always know how to effectively communicate with the ladies. Dating in your late twenties, thirties and even forties-plus is so, so incredibly more advanced in terms of individuals acumen, emotional and mental aptitude. Especially spirituality, compared to the juvenile tactics we were forced to practice and embrace during our high school and college days.

Almost every single one of us who go from being married to singlehood have largely no clue what we are doing when it comes to dating. We have been out of the "dating game" for so long that attempting to talk to other adults, especially ones we feel a sense of attraction to a member of the opposite sex seems blunderous. It occurs to me (and while all may not feel the same) that we focus so little on our strengths because we are already strong and confident in that area of ourselves, that we may treat it like a well-fortified fortress. Our psyche as "captain" if you will, is naturally inclined to "supervise" and watch over our weaknesses as they become both further exposed and more painful and less desirable to endure. We have no choice in the matter. Sure, some persons may use external substances to mask the pain that has stemmed from the exposure of our weaknesses. This is merely a stall. A temporary avoidance of the inevitable, which is the deliberate avoidance of our emotional responsibility to ourselves.

There is a word which is current and that I laugh at and embrace is "adulting". Essentially taking a noun and making it a verb by merely adding an "ing" on the end. Classic. The "adulting" thing to do is to remember why we're down here in the first place. We are here to gain experience as mortals. This obviously includes trials, tears, triumphs and victories of every kind and variety. Our end results are for us to be fitted for the Kingdom. That we could learn to choose and do so freely. So much so that the expression and the mere mention of it causes us to want to choose to come unto the Lord willingly. Oftentimes, understanding the root cause of the trial offers an eternal clarity that surpasses mere mortal understanding. It is as if, for a moment, a few crystal-clear moments, our very busy brains are temporarily shut down and we allow peace to flow through us. For that moment, we can bend, or better yet, peel back the veil and see a slight glimmer of the eternities and experience a perspective that more closely relates to Gods. A more "Eternal Perspective", as it were. These moments of clarity are the absolute height of decadence! It also allows us to feel like being part of something again. Something bigger than ourselves. Something eternal.

The Delicate Balance of Children

For those who haven't had the beautiful challenge of raising their own kids, I hope you get to have your own soon. Of the many, many things to love about kids, (my kids, particularly) is that they are always on *my side* even when they are not supposed to be. Kids in general care deeply what words are spoken *to* our former spouse and *about* our former spouse. They can get exhausted and unnecessarily worn out of feeling like they need to parent *us!* This is a very delicate and sensitive subject with more relatable facets than can be adequately expressed. I'll broach this subject delicately, quite apropos considering the subject. They're our kids. From our numerous personal parenting examples and memories that we use to pull from, we barely know what *we are* doing half the time!

Contrastingly, if we as adults keep making jokes and taking lightly our children's emotions, we may fall into a subtle trap that's designed to distance us from establishing deeper and more meaningful relationships with our children. By rummaging through this subtle practice of taking ourselves too lightly, and/or not taking seriously enough our parental responsibilities, we miss out on several plain and precious moments. These moments that can and will define the character and shaping of our little ones. It's no secret. The reality and the gravity of our kids and their feelings is of utmost importance. If we neglect and/or even avoid too many moments, these key developmental circumstances that will define us as parents will be lost. It will pass us by like a class we never took. We could miss *everything* important, *e*verything that means something to our kids and consequently and conversely, ourselves.

The next question we need to ask ourselves is: What will we do next? Or, perhaps even more compelling: What *should* we do next? If we have any real sense about ourselves, we know that answer. Step two is, and always will be, execution. Our kids deserve our best efforts. This shouldn't even be a question. As a parent of two precious children myself, I have found that there are those golden moments where being a parent is the most rewarding event that has ever transpired in my life. I'm one of the fortunate few where single parenting is literally the gift that keeps on giving. Why do I consider myself one of the "fortunate few"? Because not all fathers view and/or see their offspring the way I see my kids. It's supernal, really. I don't know how to adequately explain it; I just know that it's there. Any person, male or female can see and a sizable number have shared with me, that the relationship I share with my children is unmatched. I would biasedly agree! I'm equally fortunate enough to know and interact with other single fathers who also share a deep and profound love for their children. Watching these men is awe inspiring! Even though my relationship with my kids is as bulletproof as it is, these men further inspire me to be better. They inspire me to be better at willingly sacrificing my time, energy, funds and me to their best interests. They are as real as real can be and totally a part of me in the best and less than favorable ways. When I see similar attributes in my children (for better and for worse) it's totally endearing to me! It's bonding in an unexplainable way that is so totally compelling to me that it feigns reason and definition.

Now, the reason I relayed all that detail is for this reason, and the words which shall follow this short series of words. Children themselves are the essence of Gods Kingdom. If God's total motivation and current undertaking is solely for the bringing about the immortality and eternal life of his children, all of us, *that* should tell us where *our* priorities should be. In that of our own families and most importantly, our children. It literally breaks my heart to see and hear story after story of parents, fathers and mothers parenthetically, in so many words, neglect, dissolve and even completely avoid any real parenting responsibility! I'm not referring to the occasional "stepping out of the house" just for a moment of peace away from crying, and whining kids. I'm referring to parents avoiding and neglecting their legally scheduled visitations from their kids, basic activities such as church attendance, school activities, heck, just being a parent in any regard! These same individuals in some cases have legally signed over their paternal and maternal worldly rights and responsibilities away from their kids, and any implied responsibilities. I'm not writing these words to condemn these individuals. Nothing in this manuscript is designed or intended to "judge" any person(s) regardless of implied affronts, self-imposed, or other.

This particular chapter is meant to increase the want and desire and responsibility of being actively involved in the loving and nurturing of our children. By so doing, there may be a necessary tug at the "heart-strings" to provoke an action and hopefully several consequential actions thereafter, to be an active parent in our children's lives. To those that are already actively engaged in successful and wholesome parenting, to motivate, and inspire further activity! Too many children whom I have met, wonder what it is that they did wrong to have their parent, (mom and/or dad) neglect, avoid, or otherwise be uninterested and involved in their lives to any extent. It would do us everlastingly well to somehow embed in our children's mind that it's *not* their fault! Too many children go about their day unnecessarily with that little morsel of toxic guilt rolling around in their head about their otherwise wayward parent. The best way to counter these negative and neglectful thoughts is to *be involved in your kid's lives!* Regardless of our relationship with our ex, our relationship with our kids is so infinitely more than we can comprehend in this mortal realm. Now, I will not have anyone believe for a second that even involved parents are perfect or even any shade of perfect! We're not. I'm certainly inclined to believe that we're all striving to do our best and that one day we'll achieve that lofty goal of parenting perfection. But until then, it's the pursuit that is worth our best and most valiant effort. To the wayward parent(s) for the most part, I think I get it. There were times in my own divorce that I wanted nothing to do with anything and even anyone. I've become very acquainted with several derivations of stories and experiences where those of us parents want an escape from what's real. We want some solitude from our past and some retribution in the form of reclusiveness. I *get* that. It's not the answer you want, nor *should* you want! There is an awful hollowness in the heart and soul of the selfish person and parent. Trying to fill that hollowness with anything but being a true parent is a fool's errand. Sure, you can try to disassociate and dehumanize yourself from feeling any remaining sense of obligation and responsibility to being an involved parent. But the eternal ramifications and aftermath are not what anyone wants to endure. However, being a more involved parent strictly out of fear of eternal consequences isn't, nor will it ever be reason enough. Parenting should be entirely motivated by love! The want to see your children, to be with them, to experience their ups and downs and triumphs and successes and their disappointments is an act of love. An act of devotion. It's divine in its intent and inspired from a loving Heavenly Parent who knows ours and our children's needs, before we ask.

Defyance of Denial

"You'll be okay." That's how it goes, right? It's as if that over-inflated cliché is just the on-lookers staring down at you from some sort of self-imposed "happily married" perch or high-horse, as it were, in an attempt to try and show empathy for a situation that they will *never* understand. Let alone begin to comprehend! It's like a modest "slap in the face" quickly covered up by the blanket of their alleged friendship disguised as them "just being there for you". All the while, offering you their seemingly hollowed support. Perhaps to avoid the appearance of just not being "that guy" that casts you out into the "divorced-zone" of their circle of friends. I don't personally know if such a thing really exists, but I would imagine that if it does, it's likely worse than being "friend-zoned".

There are so many varieties of women. So much so that there are those types of women whom I haven't fallen for (in a manner of speaking) within any short (or long) periods of time. What about that one woman who threw it in with me? She took that massive leap of faith on me and what did I do? Did I do my absolute best, or did I just want what I couldn't have? Or do we just love the pursuit better than the catch? It's been said that satisfaction is the death of desire. With temporal things, and earthly accolades, and adulation from lofty eyes it can certainly be true. Temporal satisfaction begets temporal solutions to longstanding desires. We may want the latest luxury car, or the most high-tech smartphone, and that can give us that temporary "thrill of ownership", but what of the next years newer models? We lose sight of the divinity of our relationship with our spouse and other mortals, when we treat them like we do monetary replacements/upgrades.

But it's well beyond our mortal scope. I realized I can't and mustn't crucify myself over and over because of the mistakes of others. Especially my ex-spouse. I trusted her with the most sacred part of my life, my family and portions of my soul. Just because she lost sight of who she was and her familial responsibilities, doesn't justify her transgressions. It most definitely doesn't make me a "loser" either. Trusting someone to keep their end of the marital vows isn't foolish nor "looser-like". It's quite the opposite. The Adversary's best tool in this situation was (and is) my broken, bleeding, vulnerable heart and mind. And he creeps in there with his whisperings and somehow penetrates my mind and heart. The same evil voice that would have me believe that I'm unlovable. That *I* am responsible for driving my lover/spouse into the arms of another lover(s). Human or other. Meaning those spouses who were abandoned to video games, work, the pursuit of money and material possessions, the fame and honor of the Great and Spacious Building or the classic reason, a mistress or consort (male version of a 'mistress').

In a world that we can think is unchangeable, two things will always change and ironically, they are the things that impact everything else. People and perception.

Now, I know people always say that "people never change". Well that's a very finite, mortal perspective. If people never changed, then that means that the Atonement of Jesus Christ is basically useless. It's not, by the way. It's transcendent. Epic. Colossal. Suffice it to say that there are not words adequately enough to explain/describe the Master's and the Father's Everlasting Atonement.

On to the perception. Powerful and often eluding of people's most common thoughts and actions. In one instance, my significant other is everything to me. My sun, moon and stars. And with that same person, the sun rises and sets with her. I feel it. I know my heart and soul have finally found a home. Then the hammer of reality hits. Something happens. Maybe a lot of somethings happen. She starts seeing me differently. Or, sometimes, not at all. I've become as transparent to her like Dracula is in a mirror. Her perception of me changes. She starts seeing me as an emotional "liability". Her once dizzyingly euphoric perception of me falls a few too many notches. I didn't acknowledge it right away because some women for the most part are stealthy emotional killers. Sure, they'll argue with you on an occasion or two and at the time it may seem quite trivial. But every "disagreement" every time I "challenged" her opinion, told her she's wrong or perhaps even the WORST thing I could do is tell her she's "crazy". (See, women *know* they're crazy. It's just to what extent! Now, ladies, tap your brakes, men are crazy, too!) Where the important crux to connect is that each of our "brands" match we were a very good fit that way. And, IF they're YOUR "type" of crazy, which is a discussion for later.

But there she is. Your life, your love, your everything; and in one foul swoop, she's now the source of all your misery. As fate would have it, this emotional pendulum certainly swings both ways.

The Precursor

As I'm writing this book, I've preselected all my topics and subsequently assigned them all a chapter number. There really is no method to this madness, only a shot in the dark summation of what chapter sounds good or looks appropriate for whatever topic/title I feel like assigning to it.

With that said, this chapter is quite unique and special. You will find out why as you read and complete it. It starts with a novel idea - a theory. To my current knowledge, there is no Christian doctrine that I'm presently aware of to support this theory, so please allow my disclaimer that this is just a theory. They can be tested, and re-tested until proven, or eradicated.

In each and every one of our lives there exists the divine gift of agency. It's powerful. More so perhaps than gravity. It is both destiny-driven and damnation-riddled. How we use it, and even misuse it, and even how we *choose* to use it, ultimately determines our Eternal destination. The Lord has promised us the divine gift of the Holy Ghost, The Comforter. This is the Lords best influencer for us to help His children progress to Eternal Life, the greatest of all His gifts to His children. As we learn in the weekly sacramental prayer, the gift of the Holy Ghost is given to us "that they may *always* have His spirit to be with them" contingent on how we exercise our divinely gifted agency. It is truly up to us! We can do and say things that can strengthen, or weaken The Comforter's influence in our daily lives.

Elder Maxwell once stated: "So many marriages hang by a thread, or have already snapped." (Oct. 2001 General Conference) This is true because of ours and our spouse's choices. The ones we make and the ones we don't make. Sins of commission and sins of omission. We are all guilty of both. Mortality certainly provides its disadvantages! But the turning point, the turnkey is *us*. Always has been and always will be.

As we learn in 2 Nephi 9:11: "For it must needs be, that there is an opposition in all things." This is so, for more reasons than need be addressed here and now, but the direction I will use in this point is that we combat against a calculated, surgically precise, patient adversary. We underestimate him constantly, and we pay the price for our underestimations of him every single day. Any amount of spirituality that he can take from us, any number of blessings he can block from us, any amount of temptation he can throw at us he will. *Relentlessly.* Unceasingly. He won't stop until he can get us to lose so much of our ability to be spiritually sensitive and far enough away from within the protective confines of Gods spiritual fortress to the point we lose all hope in ourselves and in our spiritual self-worth to Him.

The Adversary's mission and his goal are simple. He simply is out to prove to God that the divine gift of agency is and was too much of a responsibility for the children of man to handle on our own. Ergo, his want in the premortal councils of Heaven to force all of us to do everything right, so that we could return to live with God in the highest degree of the celestial kingdom. If we look at the world today, for the most part, the adversary is unfortunately right. The majority of us children of men are running amok in total spiritual chaos! But for those of us that embrace our agency and are everlastingly working on our consummate conversion, we get to stand in the holy places of the Lord's spiritual fortress and observe the world as it metaphorically eats itself. With little to no restraint or regard for the its immediate spiritual future. The world, as it stands is mainly only interested in gratifying its own lustful and physical cravings. The natural man runs rampant and essentially gets whatever it wants, when it wants, at the selfish cost of everyone else's moral and spiritual expense. When will the world learn? It won't happen any time soon because the adversary's greatest trick is to convince the children of men that he doesn't exist. Meanwhile, systematically establishing evils that leave a destructive path in its wake. All the while, his dance of destruction and ungodliness consumes the will and agency of mankind as this diabolical show runs on autopilot.

Have you ever just had that moment of internal gravity, where you feel that you're standing still in an emotional quagmire, while the world and the people in it are fast-forwarding through life? The soul shudders in disarray. The mind weakens to the brink of collapse. The heart, as it were, willingly wishes to stop beating, perhaps in an effort (albeit a vain one) to spare us the pain of another moment in our misery. The eyes well up with what seems to be toxicity in the form of tears leaving the body. Only to still somehow leave the residual rust of the toxic memoir of what once was loving moments in a marriage, is now corroded and corrupted into moments of resounding memories of hell on earth.

There is a reason that this occurs. Sometimes it's self-inflicted. Some may even argue it's borderline masochistic. True, some of us may even feign the pain, just feel *something*; other than the gangrenous remains of a toxified relationship.

Divorce does a wicked number on those immediately involved. Of the majority, we are immediately afflicted emotionally. We have a very difficult, nigh impossible, set of both circumstances and emotions immediately thrust upon us. Anyone that is a parent of any number of kids knows that the last thing they are looking for is *more* of anything more to deal with. Sure, our families and friends will try to empathize. They'll even try to relate! Which we divorcee's will almost find vaguely insulting and borderline condescending. Not a lot of people know what it feels like, do they?! To be humiliated and rejected to the point of total disgrace. We know it. We've *felt* it - even in our bones. I mean, they "understand". Right? Even in a vain attempt to empathize, and to "understand". Our parents, relatives and friends looking on, they all "understand", for a time. But then they want the bitter divorcee' to do something we know we can't do. To "move on" right then, as if upon command, as if it's some sort of caravan to get on or off on. As if a divorce is just an emotion that we can somehow bury on the side of the unbeaten road, stake a wooden cross in the ground, made up of broken limbs from a nearby tree. Not hardly. So, after a while, everyone stops "understanding". They dismiss our broken family and broken heart and passively move us down the line of ignorant, processed emotions. It's always so much easier to deal with the emotions of an otherwise very emotional situation when it's you on the outside looking in - with no desire to venture inward. My mind registered it a little too late. We can either learn to hide the humiliation and practice smiling in the mirror and to everyone else, or we wear it more ostentatiously, causing all around us to somehow bear the proverbial burden with us. Don't be that person, because no one likes that guy.

It's so easy to want to feel sorry for ourselves during this time. Throwing our own proverbial "pity party" with seating for anyone who can pretend to be interested. It may even be temporarily comforting. But that luster fades like the polish on a missionary's shoe. It's upon this ground called "Rock-bottom" that we are given the blessed opportunity to build a better foundation and life. Why? Because it's what the "Wise Man" did in the Children's Song book! (Now you're singing it in your head!) Seriously though, why not build again at "rock bottom" and/or "Ground Zero"?

Now that we basically get to hit the "reset button" on our lives, why not make it to our every advantage? Clearly, we couldn't do so with our now ex-spouse holding us back, so why not build our own world the way we would have wanted it all along? It's not going to be easy. It never is. It's not supposed to be. There are plenty of those around us, both that we can see and are in the unseen world that would love to spiritually and emotionally and (if we let them) mentally get us down and keep us there. What I'm referring to is more – much more than the natural man. I'm talking darker, more powerful. A more diabolically personalized approach. I'm referring to everyone's spiritual "Anti-self". Now, for the theoretical emphasis on the chapter. This is going to be good.

The Dark Side of Mortal Agency

When the one-third of the hosts of heaven foolishly chose to follow the Dark Prince, they made their proverbial bed, and they'll forever have to sleep in it. Although they are eternally spirits, dark entities - as it were - they don't *need* sleep per se. These dark entities will never have a physical body; ergo they don't need to rest. They don't stop planning, plotting, scheming the best and most effective ways to destroy us. They will stop at nothing to tear us down, to drive us as far away from our Heavenly Father and Savior as they can. We all know that the evil in the world is authored by the Dark Prince. Elder Jeffrey R. Holland referenced the Dark One and put it rather astutely: "We don't talk about the adversary any more than we have to and I don't like talking about him at all… Number one, Satan, or Lucifer, or the father of lies— call him what you will—is real, the very personification of evil. His motives are in every case malicious and he convulses at the appearance of redeeming light, at the very thought of truth. Number two, he is eternally opposed to the love of God, the Atonement of Jesus Christ and the work of peace and salvation. He will fight against these whenever and wherever he can. He knows he will be defeated and cast out in the end, but he is determined to take down with him as many others as he possibly can." (October 2011 General Conference). My strongest suggestion to you the reader is: Know the difference, and know the type! Don't be one of the fallen! Lucifer *has targeted me* through my ex, as an effort to tear me down as well! He has tried, and tried, time and time again with me. He's won a few battles, but as the small battles wage on, he'll never win the war, if you pick up what I'm putting down.

One of the best pawns that the Dark Prince will use incessantly to take us down, is what I like to theorize, and call (in my case) is the "Anti-Ryan". It is the dark entity version of me. My unseen, spiritual opposite. It knows me the same, if not better than I even do myself. It knows my weaknesses, my strengths, the chinks in my spiritual armor. It's the messenger and deliverer of all my various temptations, and it's #1 goal is to drag me to hell along with himself.

Pretty daunting, eh? It's as if, in these last days, that there are those of us that have such unique missions in this life that we are supposed to accomplish, some divine end-game, as it were, that Gods needs each one of us to accomplish individually. Not just for the gospel cause itself, but in addition to our own refinement, to continue us on the path of our own conversion. It makes sense, doesn't it? I mean, haven't you, the reader, ever just felt that there are some trials, some temptations that are thrown at you that have been so well-devised, so expertly conceived that as the Dark Prince is "winding up" (so to speak) that he just *knows* that this will greatly affect your immediate and in his eyes, your long-term spiritual destination? I know I have. Sure, I've been hit with a few of those proverbial pitches, as well. But I know in whom I've trusted. It never matters the speed of the pitch the Adversary has thrown at you. It never matters how hard it may or may not hit you. It doesn't even matter the damage the impact of the pitch has done. If we're living our lives right (at least as right as we can), and maintaining the whole armor of God as our garb, the Atonement can and will renew any damage of the impact Lucifer's fastball(s) may have on us. This so aptly applies to our individual lives, as well as our married, and divorced and single lives.

So, we face this dark entity of ours that I hypothesize of in a 24/7-day format. Day in, day out, in our awake, and even our sleeping states. It may seem that they have a sizable advantage over us, as they do not require sleep due to the lack of a physical body. So, they are always conscious of us (in one form or another) and our realities, and their main goal of destroying us. Great news is, help is available! A woman by the name of Sharon G. Larson, said in the October 2001 General Conference: Elisha the Prophet was surrounded by the whole Syrian army determined to kill him…that when we are on the Lord's side, regardless of numbers or worldly power, we are in the majority…"They that be with us are more than they that be with them" (2 Kgs. 6:16).

The times that I really focus hard on the Eternal Perspective, the gift the Lord so desperately wants all of us to not only receive, but to use it early and often like each breath we take. It's as if I can see him. Sense him, almost feel his dark presence. The Anti-Ryan. I feel that he's mocking my knowledge of his awareness even as I type these words. He's arrogant, prideful, selfish, degenerate, lethal, and spiritually toxic. Oh, I know him, and I am very aware *of* him. He hates my every breath. He loathes my every good deed. Every time I've used and continue to use the priesthood of God to bless someone else, he's waiting in an adjacent room, frustrated and upset that he's losing the battle for my soul and agency. I love upsetting him; and even offending him, often and frequently. Be careful, and ever so mindful of this type of disposition, because we should not perform these offending deeds just to spite him, that's the wrong reason and equally wrong motivation. The real reason we would be well to perform these good deeds, these acts of service is with the intent and motivation to serve the Lord with the right "heart, might, mind, and strength", (D&C 4:2). Service to the Lord is to be done and executed because we love Him, and that we want to serve Him. Pure, plain, and simple. It all boils down to choice. We are free to choose our actions, but not the consequences. Interesting to consider, most every sin we commit, usually has something to do with violating someone else's agency. An act that infringes on the agency of another (and/or others).

It may seem like a most daunting task to oppose such a dark concept. There are those that may disagree that such a dark entity even may exist. There's no proof on either side of that debate. Consider the alternative, wouldn't the Dark Prince do everything in his power to try and prove that he's right? Wouldn't he fight his finest fight? Wouldn't he fire everything he's got at us just to laugh at us while he watches us fall? That sounds exactly like the thinking of an enemy to me. This wouldn't be an actual *physical* fall per se, but a spiritual one. A moral, emotional, and diabolical fall. If "Adam fell, that men might be, and men are that they might have joy", and the Dark Prince is the literal opposite, the literal manifest destiny of evil, and spiritual distortion. Then his deployment of any and all means necessary to drag us down to hell with him makes clarion sense. So why do we *let* him? Why do we allow ourselves to give into temptation? Why do we insist on persisting in sin? I feel the answer is rooted deeply with in us. We are spiritual children of a loving God who knows what we need, even before we ask! Do we ask to be delivered from evil? Or do we have a casual, more nonchalant approach with our discipleship? The answer (as I suggested earlier) is our conversion, or rather, where we are, (or are not) in our own conversion. Conversion isn't just a decision to start doing what's right. It's not even the first 10 good decisions. Sure, those previous steps are all components to a converted soul, but ultimately don't produce an actual "conversion" necessary to be well on one's way to conversion.

So what are some of the ways that we all can counter our spiritual opposite? Our own individual "Anti-Ryan"? Elder Maxwell offers some great counsel: "The best way to 'put off the [Anti-Ryan] is to starve him. Weakened, he is more easily dislodged.

Otherwise he insists on getting his 'ticket punched' on every stop on the temptation train." (Seventh Commandment; a Shield, October 2001 General Conference). The more correct, and spiritually-guided decisions we make, the closer we draw to God and our Savior. The closer we draw to them, the easier it is to continue to follow them. The same can be said of our disobedience. If we do not discipline our habits and desires to match the Lords standards, we will find ourselves distancing our souls from the Lord that created us. That same Creator wants nothing more than for us to be happy the way He defines it. He does, after all, know everything, so you'd think we'd be a bit more compliant to His will. Mortality is not without its inherent propensity for disobedience. All is never lost, when we know who the winning side is going to be, and we would do well to choose that side for ourselves.

The Dark Side has a way of molding us, if we allow it. Just like we have the power to turn a trial into a strength, we can extract the dark side of a trial, and use that experience, that struggle to elevate us. That's the whole design of the trial, isn't it? If we examine that word, and for more of its literal meaning, "trial" is in essence, a test of the performance, qualities, or suitability of someone or something. Our character is a byproduct of our trials. We are the literal result and personification of our spiritual training. The key to that dark side in ourselves is that we cannot fall victim to its intentions. We must pass through the darkest of clouds, or "mists" as it were, with our hands firmly on the iron rod, as the one "constant" that is always there leading to higher ground. Trials, as we recognize, are not necessarily a form of punishment for past sins. Quite the opposite. Joseph Smith and most every prophet before and after him went through more trials than some may argue that he should have. But he endured them nonetheless. Trials are never about fairness. It's more about being better prepared for the days, and weeks and months ahead. Trials will never stop. They never take a day off, they never rest, they are precisely scheduled, and almost totally unpredictable by nature. Why is this some ask? My suggestion is that God needs us to "stay on our toes". We as Gods' best children are constantly getting better at managing trials and tribulations, and even better, we are never expecting our trials, but we may find ourselves unexpectedly prepared for it. One may ask: "Okay, then how does one "prepare" for trials, and tribulations? Diligence in gospel basics. Reading, studying, and pondering the scriptures. Saying heartfelt, meaningful prayers with the diligence God requires. Temple attendance, tithing, etc.. Okay, okay, you're saying…we get it. The best news is, we don't even have to *be ready* for them! God will prepare us for the trials and tribulations ahead of us. If we are prepared we won't need to fear what may come next. Especially in terms of the "curve balls" that our exes may or may not throw at us.

The Perpetuity of "Why"

The scriptures remind me early and often the main point of my existence. Why I'm down here. Why I experience pain, pleasure, sadness, happiness, health, and sickness, and so on. I get to experience it in all its many forms, and types. It's never going to get easy. My resistance to trials will be strengthened if I make a habit out of learning what I'm supposed to from the trials that I encounter, endure, and conquer. What I was curious to know is, am I using my trials to develop godly character? Am I "enduring to the end" as the scriptures command? Am I anxiously engaged in *that* good cause? OUR cause? I hope so. I for one, have found myself guilty on more than one occasion bellyaching to the Lord about my certain set of circumstances, relationship, divorce, or other, only to be perpetually reproved, delicately chastened, lovingly reprimanded, and send on my mortal way. There's nothing pleasant about it. It's a *proving* process for all of us. I not only need to prove myself to the Lord often and frequently, but I need to prove my character to *myself*. It's like paleontology, and/ or archeology, after I do the necessary "digging", then, and only then, am I rewarded for my efforts. It's also not always the reward that I'm expecting. It occurs to me, that in the darkest hours, in the worst times of our lives, if I will stop feeling sorry for myself, and utilize the Eternal Perspective a little, I can truly see myself the way my loving Heavenly Father, and his Son, our elder Brother do. With divine potential. With pride, *godly* pride, mind you. With the foresight recognition that "…all these things shall be but a small moment…" and if I then, in turn, trust God, and His timing, and His grace, He will carve out the former natural man inside of me. As a result, He will replace that void with a greater portion of the Divine Nature that I so desperately need. But, almost ironically enough, I may have otherwise rejected because of the "mighty change" that is required of all of us disciples. This is required to progress, in order to more fully embrace the entirety of the Divine Nature, and gradually build a god-like life. This mighty change doesn't come about because I ask it to, but because I earn it, to some relative extent. It becomes my character. Consider the exact phrasing: "Mighty". This type of change doesn't come easy. Nothing great or "Mighty" in this case will come easy. If it does, it isn't worth having. If it doesn't then work at it until the prize is yours!

It all works out, you see. I don't say that with any sort of triteness, but more so that we can better understand the magnitude and gravity of the possibilities, the *Eternal* possibilities. Sure, it's super easy to get down on ourselves over the more rippling drama that seems to resonate in our lives. But there is godly hope and wisdom in this realm. Picture this: If we literally went through our lives un-tempted, unproven, untested, unshaken, and care-free, would we have the audacity, the gumption - as it were - to face our Maker saying we "deserve" to join the company of the spiritual "greats", namely Nephi, Alma, Moses, Noah, Captain Moroni, Brigham Young, David O. McKay, etc.,? We *have* to be honest with ourselves when we answer that question. I, nor anyone else, couldn't take someone seriously if they claimed such. Here comes the eternal perspective to describe this concept: Too much peace will weakens us. Too much peace in between trials can cause us to weaken our loyalties; not just to ourselves in our character, but to our developing discipleship to the Lord. Not just physically, in terms of exercise, and being active, but it also applies to our spiritual faculties as well. If we rest for too long, or have a lengthy period where we go trial-less, we can slowly embrace the false notion that all is well. We can begin to fool ourselves that with everything being just right in our life, that we start thinking "what could possibly go wrong?" mentality. See, this is dangerous thinking and a harmful disposition for many reasons. We'll address some, if not most of them here. When something finally *does* go wrong, it can cause us to go into an immediate panic. That's our emotional side exaggerating the circumstance for our lack of present and situational-awareness. Very few good decisions have ever occurred when we panic. We can turn to fault-finding, in an effort to stave off the blame on ourselves and find some sort of excuse, some scapegoat, as it were, to blame so that our internal guilt and conscience are, for the moment, pacified. We can do, say, act in a way that can most assuredly make any negative situation worse. That's never cool. Then, finally, there's our timeless, overused friend, "denial". I endured its company for a time early on in my divorce. I was convinced that everything was entirely everyone else's fault, and I lacked the courage to accept responsibility and take ownership of my multiple shortcomings. I did so many stupid things. No doubt, they were shamefully conceived, and poorly executed. I shared more mental "bandwidth" with denial than anyone ever should, and as a result I lost sight for a time as to who I was as a man, as a father, as a son, and as a brother, and as a friend. Denial is parallel to selfishness. It only serves itself, with the hopes of further blinding its host, *us*. See, *we* feed the demons, and/or angels that we give mindshare to in our heads, hearts, and soul. But the best thing I (eventually) did was "man up" and challenged myself to step up and become man enough (to a greater degree, anyway) face and confront my issues, and consequently conquer them. It was only then that after I was both destroyed, and/or allowed myself to be destroyed, that I was then allowed to fix myself. Reinvent myself as it were. It's a process, a delicate one. I always knew the proverbial pieces of myself always "fit", per se. But it was in the process of putting the pieces of myself back together that I found that I could build upon what I already had to work with. I could, and still can build myself any way I wanted. But this time, I wanted the Lord's help. Now, don't get me wrong, if there were some device that could let you the reader see into my internal "Construction Site" you'd see signs all over warning of "Caution Hard-hat area, proper safety gear is required on or near site". Or, however construction site signs are worded. Mine reads something very close to that. My point is, that I'm still eons away from any semblance of a "finished product". The good news is, I'm still "underway" as opposed to "delayed" or "project terminated".

The other facet to strongly consider is the fact that a "victorious mentality" can be helpful, but we mustn't rest on our laurels. Ever. This is brewing grounds for some of the dark prince's finest, most subtle work. Victory doesn't always favor the winning team. That may sound pretty confusing, but allow me to explain. Victory is and most certainly can be an abstract concept. It is impartial, uncommittable, and can, and will pivot over the most inconsequential mistakes. Just because you've embraced victory once, doesn't assure, or guarantee you'll ever see it, experience it, or even embrace it ever again. That's both the advantage and disadvantage of its abstract nature. It's intangible, immaterial nature is also what makes it so sought after, and also so discouraging. Simply put, victory, it all its shapes and forms can, in turn, defeat us. So much success, or even too much of it can cause complacency. We can come to expect victory just by showing up, or by a self-inflated sense of entitlement. Victory, like the love of a spouse, must be constantly earned. Ever pursued, ever sought-after, and evermore desired, victory is to be achieved and will be under the proper motivation, which is the love and approval of our Savior and Heavenly Father. With that motivation, and real intent, we will draw closer to

Heavenly Father, our Savior and our own Divine Nature. Even more importantly, become the person, the son or daughter of God that the Lord needs and wants us to be. The only obstacle we'll ever face – is *ourselves*. The dark version of us. The voice in our heads that we've earlier identified as the "Anti-[insert readers name]", that tells us that exaltation is a pipe dream. That we're far too imperfect to ever live with God and his holy Son and prophets and all those that currently, and will someday enjoy the Celestial experience. Now that we know the evil influence inside of us and it's source, it's up to us to fight back. To fight *it* back. Don't worry about tools or weapons, we are already armed. We'll always be undergoing our "training". Don't just uncover your demons, dissect them so you can find out what they've been feeding on. Go out there and give it our best, and let God and his angels make up the rest.

Advice of Others

People share with me their advice on a rather uncanny, and unsolicited routine basis about my situation, and circumstance, as (now get this—) it pertains to them. This provides a window of humor for me. I don't mean that in a patronizing, condescending way at all. I can find humor in most any given set of unfortunate and fortunate circumstances. I can find the snow in the proverbial dirt storm. Why I find this particular offering of advice humorous is that it's coming from my currently married friends. Most any divorcee` that you may talk to will agree. Marriage, and/or relationship advice from a married person to a divorcee` is like the "Armchair Quarterback". AFTER the play has been executed, (albeit poorly, for this example's sake) the "Armchair Quarterback" has the luxury of saying: "Oh, jeepers! I would have "zigged" where that player "zagged" right there…!" Or: "Next time they run that play again, they need to have the receiver run a post rout…" or, whatever post-play perspective comment the ACQB (Armchair Quarterback) feels like regurgitating. So it is with our married friends with the sound relationship advice. Just like God will force no man to heaven, we cannot force our spouses to love us, stay true to us, stay true to the gospel, nor, force them to live up to their role within the family you've created together. Agency, is always in play, and very healthy as well. There's nothing you and I can do or say to alter agency, nor its role in the divine eternal perspective of things.

One of the things that some of my married and perpetually single friends will volunteer to me in the form of advice, laced with empathy, is: "Oh, whoa, you're a single parent! You must know a lot about sacrifice!" Which isn't too far from the *actual* truth. Now, don't get me wrong, these onlookers mean well. They mean very well. It's my perspective that it's no real sacrifice, per se. Sacrifice, to me, precludes a choice that needs to be made. One can *choose* to give up something. That's sacrifice. Depending on my audience, I will make a follow-up statement to that initial insight.

I counter with: "I'm much more familiar with "loss". This reference to "loss" is when other people's choices negatively affected me.

This isn't a negative disposition at all. It's a grounded, down-to-earth, realist point of view. Sure losses (as I've chosen to define it in this example) of many kinds and degrees have negatively affected everyone that has ever lived. I'm certainly not on any exempt list for "loss". My losses have just, on a more personal level to me, negatively affected my immediate family and loved ones. It's life. I'd love to shake hands with the person who claims that life has totally gone according to plan for them, and publicly congratulate them. I'm grateful that I've never have to make such an ostentatious act. What I've learned, and what I wish I knew earlier on in life after divorce, is that one cannot let their struggles and trials, and troubles *define* them. It's so easy to accept the self-damaging, and depressing disposition of victimization of oneself. Don't be that person. We are always stronger, and more capable than our trials, and temptations.

Speaking of facing temptations and trials, where we face a very capable and very aggressive opponent in our own opposition is that we are facing a time and present-day where relationships are harder now than they ever have been before. So many of us "walking-wounded" are still "in it". Which, I realize is a very subjective term. It's safe to say, that the same number of persons are only hanging on by a very thin thread, if only because we have to. I mean, what other choice do we have? It seems as though, that if we're not in the gospel, striving, living it, and trying to stay obedient to the degree we can, then we're in something else's power. There is no "middle ground" contrary to what the majority may suggest. We're either in the gospel or we're not. Discipleship in the Lords Kingdom isn't, nor should be conditional. Especially on our limited, and mortal conditions, and terms, as if we had any real power to suggest to the Lord otherwise. So we continue to hang on to this very thin thread. How do we strengthen this thread? It's important to note what is symptomatic of a "thin rope". The vast majority of the time, this thin rope is dangling so helplessly because of external factors that can, and often do affect us emotionally, and mentally. Whether it ranges from past relationship disappointments ranging from heartbreaks, to being forgotten about, left out whether intentionally, or accidentally, to being emotionally mistreated, and abused, to ultimate spousal betrayal. Pick one. Or several. Or all. When the end result is the same, it doesn't matter what the cause is. The only factor that remains is finding the cure.

I can't expect anyone to understand. Sure there may be a handful of us divorcee's out there that can relate, but married persons with kids will simply never understand. They'll never understand what it's like to be missed so badly by their own children, to be so close, yet so far away from them by a few cities, and state lines, and in some cases, across national borders and overseas. To miss them right back, but to have the emotional wherewithal to pause your heart. Now, don't mistake, this isn't numbing oneself so they can't/don't feel the "hurt/miss", but rather an emotional defense mechanism as a result of so much pain for such a long time. As it stands, for every divorce, or breakup, we add one or more emotional "lock" to the door of our hearts. Normally, I'd say an expression like "an extended period of time" but that seems like a discredit, and a mockery of the emotions. What exactly *is* an "extended period of time" when it comes to matters of the heart? It's clearly undefined, as there is just nothing to measure it too. So we take the next step and make the next advancement to the lack of understanding of married person's with kids. In a few circumstances I've experienced, I've left my daughters in the capable care of their grandparents while I go to work, or some other obligation. As I hold them, and kiss them, and whisper the most positive of encouragements, in their loving, and receptive ear, I almost feel compelled to say a goodbye like it's the last time I'm going to see them. Although, there may be a small sliver of truth to that statement, it still breaks my heart to think it. To think in my protective "Poppa Bear" mind, that they will be suddenly so far out of my protective reach, and away from me hearing the sounds of their cries for help, (even if it's just in my mind) shatters me.

It's true I live in a world that so few could ever, ever understand, let alone even fewer could ever *exist* in, that it's reasonably unspeakable. It's times like this when I vehemently emphasize that I do not advocate divorce. The misleading concept that surrounds the term "divorce" like a deceptive mist that makes it so hard to realize is that it's actually a viable answer to what may otherwise be a unanswerable conundrum. There's nothing easy about marriage. Even the seemingly happiest of couples will not lie to us and tell us that everything always is easy. They certainly won't tell us solutions to disagreements and family matters are as easily found as the daisies in their front yard flower bed. This isn't Stepford. It's barely "Happy Valley" (the Utah one, not in Pennsylvania). The right kind of woman doesn't want you to be the perfect guy. She just wants honesty. Honesty in the right circumstantial context is a huge mental turn on for women. At first, I didn't know to what extent, or even to whatever degree. What I now understand (better late than never) is that women just want to be told the truth, but not just for the sake of honesty. Perhaps sometimes it is that reason, but in this example, women would rather have two hard truths, than one lie, *every time*. I was not surprised by this concept but an apt, eager learner. I further inquired. I asked another female friend why exactly lies are so emotionally and mentally hurtful to her, and women in general. Her answer vexed me so that I was ashamed I didn't realize this truth sooner. She said: "Lies hurt so deeply and profoundly because it makes me feel like I'm not worth the truth." Yikes. That struck such a solid cord in me, that I not only redefined the term "lying" to myself, but I also know now what I need to do and say when it comes to my communications with others; Especially women. Let me be clear. Lying is *never* acceptable. There's an unusual sense of code inside each guy (and perhaps women as well) that can, on the rare case-by-case- situation rationalize telling a little white lie. Guys can justify (again, it doesn't make it right) a lie for a variety of different reasons I'll explain in a few later paragraphs. While honesty can seem sometimes like it only exist on the same island as Unicorns, and Dragons, most often times in our mortal communications, the most effective bridge to effectively build relationships is honesty. It's so mission-critical, that everything else is dependent on honesty. Don't believe me? Try having a healthy, thriving relationship without it. We men need to understand and embrace that we *need* to be man enough to face and communicate with our women with the reality that she's so very deserving of the truth.

Learning to Love Again

What set of circumstances would have to exist in order to love someone again? Seems like a daunting task to any of us that have been divorced, broken up with, dumped or otherwise separated from a former love. It's a dark corner of our heart and mind to want to even approach. To some, it's bigger than any elephant, or gorilla, or any other larger than life-sized animal that can be personified into an adult-level problem. I mean, everybody wants their "somebody", right? It's why most songs are written, it's why most movies are made. It's why we fall in love in the first place. It's why we throw caution into the wind. It's why we like, and even love someone more than we like or even love ourselves. Then we jump. Willingly jump into this vat of chemically-enhanced hormone-driven, subconsciously-inspired "plunge" as it were, and we try and make a relationship out of it. In this process, we ask ourselves, is this person *worth* the potential heartbreak (supposing that there might be one)? Because of the inevitability of one of two outcomes: Marriage, or break up. There's no other way to look at it. Some of you might say: *"But what about my "on again, off again" relationship with 'person xyz'?* To which I reply, depending on who's really on again, and off again, you/they're just plain old not into you enough to commit. That topic alone is another circus, and another barrel of monkey's right there.

This is a "is this person WORTH taking the chance again?" The criteria and outline for love and courtship would suggest a resounding "YES!" If our ultimate goal is happiness in a relationship, then there are two sides to the proverbial coin. We have to both be willing to have our heart broken by this person, and be able to jump into a relationship. Because if you're meant to be together, then each of your respective "crazy" will play well with each other! That's the makings of a happy-crazy, or a crazy-happy relationship and/or marriage! We just never know what specific lessons that we're supposed to learn from each other to either grow and progress ourselves closer to our Heavenly Father. You may also learn something important from the other person to grow and mature yourself in a way that the other person needed to and you needed to, and there was no other way for that message and or experience to transpire, and spiritually, emotionally, or mentally mature to our ultimate goal: Both marriage and returning to live with Heavenly Father again. We have to be open to heartbreak. It may sound borderline masochistic, but by being open to heartbreak, we equally need to be open to learning the lessons that come along with each relationship.

Now, we need to be careful with this. Just as everything has its opposite, this also applies to the messages the dark prince loves to send our way. When God sends us a lesson of love, the enemy of our souls can convolute the lesson prematurely with messages of doubt and distortion. He can, if we allow him, to believe that the lessons we're supposed to learn are that we are to just give up. That heartbreak is too hard, and too painful, and no guy or girl or prospective family situation is worth the pain and suffering of these lessons of love. This is an obvious lie. It *is* worth it. Every time, with every person we meet and take a chance on. Lessons learned transform into testimony-building experiences whose byproduct is us drawing closer to God.

As much as we may not recognize it, we all impact each other's lives with our day-to-day interactions. Granted, they may not be as profound and pivotal as a real life-altering moment, but little subtle changes are in effect constantly. God loves us. He watches over us. He traditionally meets our needs through others and gives them opportunities to serve not only to bless their lives, but most importantly, so that we can bless each other's lives, and benefit from others acts of service and want to pass that on to others. Service is everlasting. God is already in His heaven, as we are all very well aware, and even He still serves.

See? It *does* all work out in the end. If it hasn't worked out for you yet, then it isn't the end.

So, I shift directions a little, and ask myself: "At what point, does "unconditional love" become "conditional"? How much infidelity, abuse, and other heinous acts transform what was, (or at least supposed to be) unconditional? I ask because, one doesn't do such heinous acts to someone they love. So when the temptations are acted upon, are we just left to our own devices to see how much we can, or want to tolerate before we leave a relationship? I once heard a brokenhearted victim that endured severe betrayal in their marriage on multiple levels once tell me this drop of wisdom: "People talk of unconditional love, but love ends at betrayal." Seems like a bleak yet logical prospect. I also understand this completely. I can even personally empathize. For the relationship that ends unceremoniously, and rather tepidly, who am I to argue that point? Seems too pretentious; yes, even for me.

So what then, is to be done? Some people can rationalize that their divorce was a wonderful thing, and it liberated them in some emotional or mental form. That could very well be true. These sorts of experiences are usually very circumstantial and case-by-case. These same people have expressed that they feel that once they'd realize it's all behind you all the bitterness and anguish and torments that it somehow erases itself. I don't know if that's the passive aggressive approach, or just merely burying the hatchet, with handle throat, still exposed to the elements, in so many words. Perhaps it's simply just a matter of heart. Or, consequently, *lack thereof.* In either case, for those of us that have been on the other side of that coin it wasn't like that for us. It's like having a gaping legal hole torn in our universe. Some would say that's because we've never really let anything go as far as the bitterness, fear, and hatred and especially the pain, and think, there's some truth to that. Then on the other side of that coin, it wasn't like that for us. It's like having a giant hole ripped in our universe has someone say that's because we never really let anything go as far as the bitterness fear hatred especially the pain. If you think about it there's some truth to that because it's the pain that holds people together I also test the parts, the need to hurt another person once they're gone there's nothing left. Nothing worth saving anyway. That's just one jaded opinion, it's a case-by-case basis everyone's different, but I have to believe there's some truth to that. Once are able to let go of the hate, love can replace and cancel out the anger and the hate.

Some possess this all-too-rare ability to be with, and to remain in a relationship with someone despite the maltreatment of their partner; Or maybe in spite of it. In either case, are we, in fact, with this chosen, yet entitled generation of singles doomed to determine our own relationship status fate? Seems like a pejorative term when stated that way. I submit we do not face so bleak of a prospect. What is the answer some; if not most of you readers will ask? It's simple, really. Like most brilliant solutions, it's simple. The only real preventative is *us.* Our agency. This is not the proposed solution; mind you, just a means to an end. So here is the solution: Vulnerability. It is the key that we need the most to thrive in relationships, and consequently, the emotional element that is most likely the first element that we as single persons shut off to possible suitors, and prospective partners. So we "fake it till we make it." Subconsciously putting on the façade that we're emotionally available, ergo ready for the next chance and possibility of a relationship. This act that we put on can be so good that we may often time fool ourselves. I know I'm guilty of it. But I didn't care. Still don't! I had to be in an emotionally dark place to make certain decisions that eventually led to levels of demise that I was admittedly not prepared for. Some of them were in the form of relationships gone bad, some of them were in the form of decisions I would wait some time to face the consequences of. These came in the form of offended parties both directly, and indirectly of persons of whom my poor decisions directly influenced, and in some cases, affected. I didn't allow myself to be vulnerable. I was closed off, and intentionally emotionally unavailable. I was able to fool myself into thinking that I was "okay". That I was still emotionally "on the mend" and therefore able to pick my proverbial "grieving process" and that would allow me to achieve that most-desired goal of emotional availability. What I learned about this process, (and it was a lengthy one) is that I shouldn't choose my grieving process without professional guidance. "Why" might some of you ask? Because, if you'll recall a few pages ago, my reference to our own "Anti-spiritual Self" that is literally waiting in the wings, as it were, with the perfect formula and plan to trick us into thinking that what we need in order to heal, is exactly the path the adversary wants us to take. This so he can strike us at the precise worst moments of our greatest weaknesses and slowly, desensitize us, draw us away from the comfort and protection of our Heavenly Father, and spiritually drag us down to hell on earth. The Devil will always require his "pound of spiritual flesh", but it's up to us to either resist his temptations, or give in to him, and then be in his power.

So we need to choose to allow ourselves to become vulnerable. The literal definition of "vulnerable" suggests that in order for one to be truly "vulnerable", we need to be "susceptible to physical or emotional attack or harm". Now, let's further examine this claim. Note that the definition starts with the adjective "susceptible". Not "definitely be hurt" or "you will most definitely be harmed", just "susceptible". Yes, there is risk involved. Relationships are *not* for the faint of heart, but they are for the *willing* heart. There are no guarantees in the game of love and relationships. It's true, that the odds may seem against us. But honestly reader, please tell me what activity, what commitment, what worthwhile pursuit that is out there that doesn't require some risk? Your answer is *nothing*. Nothing that is worthwhile comes easy, or doesn't involve some level of risk. In the more optimistic perspective, isn't that what makes it so much fun?! Honestly, evaluate that conjecture. Dating is, in and of itself an exhausting, ever-present, necessary evil. It is. It's almost like it should be regulated on a highly concentrated level of command. Imagine that, "communist dating". Yeah, right! Not happening!

Now, think about it. Dating, at least the pursuit of finding the person with whom you can be compatible, and maybe even the most compatible, is a great time! It's loaded with intrigue, with suspense, with unpredictable twists and plot-turns, (this description is starting to sound like a Hollywood movie pitch!) and best of all, it will have a happy conclusion! Dating is exhausting, but the journey can and should be exciting! As an adult, we can see the world much clearer, and consequently more cynical. This serves both good and bad purposes. The bad is that we can let the negativity of past relationships, and heartbreaks determine how long we choose to not be vulnerable and not let someone who would have been a great match for us – in. Then, once that person, that opportunity is missed has vanished, we can then be haunted by their memory of "the one that got away".

Don't make this mistake. The false concept of "Soul Mates" is a fairy tale and a pipe-dream of exponential proportions. How can we be so sure? Because of God's Omniscience. He not only has seen the end from the beginning in every facet of our lives, but most importantly, He's made ample provisions. Included in His "ample provisions" is the divine reassurance that He has contingencies for every necessary instance and circumstance worthy of His divine intervention. The more difficult part about that with us mortals is that we can't and haven't seen the end from the beginning through the Makers eyes. Which is where faith comes in. We simply could not believe in, fully trust, and help build the Kingdom with an alleged "Supreme Being" that doesn't know everything! Now, because our Heavenly Father does know all things, we *can* trust Him. Which is also to say that we are required to trust His timing. There is always a reason behind our trials. There's always a "Spiritual Polishing" in the form of a trial, trouble, or tribulation. It's one of the ways God gets us to trust Him. We simply need to involve Him.

Soul Mates, or Fate Intervenes?

I shared a deep and provocative conversation with a female friend of mine when the topic (inevitably) surfaced about "Soul Mates". While I personally do not believe that Soul Mates exist, the conversation always sparks personal insight. And, well, I simply cannot resist some introspection! Said she: "I wish there really was such a thing as a soulmate. Why didn't Heavenly Father make us that way? When we found our soul mate are our mind heart soul and body just connected with the other person. Wouldn't that be awesome?"

I surprised myself with my reply:

"The concept of a "Soul Mate" is too fantastical. It takes away our agency. If we knew that someone was meant for us, we wouldn't have a choice."

Agency is so important, so mission critical. So much so that a war was fought in the premortal existence, in a place predominantly peaceful, and full of love and tranquility over agency.

So do that. Involve Him, early and often and frequently.

Now, for the good side of vulnerability (you may have thought I had forgotten, didn't you?)

The good is that we can take the bad and good results of past experiences, and do what we should do with all our conquered trials, and that is - *learn from them*. Take what you have learned, gained, and your character strengths, and apply what you now know, and knowledge you've been awarded with and use it to better your next relationship(s). That's part of the amazing sequence that I've endured well, is that my next (and final) relationship and marriage is going to be infinitely stronger and more protected now that I've seen the world through both heaven's and hells eyes. I want this for all of you readers. So badly, I do. So much so, that this diatribe is being written so that in some way, we can inspire, and strengthen each other, and further prevent divorce, and the downfall of the sanctity of marriage both civilly and eternally.

The Everso Lingering Dark Side

This is going to get dark. Before I cross into this realm, I want to make this one item, this one simple comparison clear. I believe there is a difference between "dark" and "evil". Both can be considered basically cousins in terms of the realms that they occupy. But I don't engage too much with "evil". I've witnessed its powers, its profound influence, and most importantly, its perpetual tendency to never have any light, nor anything positive come as a direct result of its influence and involvement. It's just not to be trifled with. Darkness. The mere void of light, from a physics perspective. That's the direction we'll go. Think of this more of a literary tour in a guarded, protected atmosphere, where we the journeymen and women and verbal adventurists are safeguarded, but have a 360-degree view encompassed by a protected, motorized orb. We'll have full autonomy in the directions we'll go.

I'll offer this positive disclaimer that I'll complete this chapter already having determined and decided that I'm on the Lords side. We are going to explore exactly how, we can use our individual "dark side" for good. Intrigued? Me too. Here we go…

It is written in 2 Nephi 9 that "there must be opposition in all things". (2 Nephi 9:11) We simply cannot fully enjoy that which is good, great, healthy, delicious, pleasing, and satisfying without having an understanding, albeit a personal understanding, of each of those adjectives *opposites*. Which makes perfect sense, if we think about it. We cannot know what it's like to fully appreciate our health, if we've never been sick, or experienced an illness. We cannot fully know how delicious a glass of chocolate milk is, without having tasted sour or spoiled milk. Just like we cannot know what a good marriage, and good relationship is, if we've never been in, or had a bad one (or two, or three, or several). Most, if not all of us have experienced some form of a relationship. They all ebb and flow, peaks and valleys, highs and lows. Sadly, in most cases, it takes one little thing, one (seemingly) tiny offense, and it can explode like a box full of TNT with a very, very short fuse. If the debris clears and you're left standing there with your eyebrows singed, and the hair on your head looks like the aftermath of a warzone, then be lucky you're still standing. Initially, it may seem like the shine is off the proverbial apple. For us guys it can quickly come to realize that – that pretty little girl that's supposed to be yours for time and eternity, or till death do you part, *isn't* so pretty on the inside. Or so it would seem. She's now (In this case and instance) taken on the form of a guy's greatest fear, as a man-eater. And, no, not the classic song from Hall & Oats, but the kind that uses a man's dignity as a disposable rag normally used to clean up vomit, etc.. Now, guys, this isn't to say that we haven't both intentionally and unintentionally provoked her from time to time. Us guys thinking and even rationalizing away some of our less-than-intelligent, and less than thought-through actions and antics. It exists in most if not all relationships that we can and often do take for granted our spouse, and their unconditional love for us. We unintentionally and intentionally act out and even say things we know we shouldn't, and oftentimes we don't even mean, because we're in this mindset of disgruntled entitlement. Because we know, in the end, they'll still be our spouse. This mindset and eventual acting out has been the gateway for so many marriages that are either ending, hang by a thread, or have already snapped. It's always the little things, that snowball to the big, and bigger things that blow everything up.

Honestly, that's what a marriage is, right? Two people that are so hell-bent on having each other's backs that they are viciously, and inescapably committed and loyal, that the Dark Prince *has* to meddle. It's just what he does. He sees two people in an otherwise very happy and loving relationship, and he, looking on, from his hellish perch says under his breath, "Challenge accepted".

We know it's supposed to be a marriage. We know it's supposed to be hard, and great, and loving and tumultuous and rocky, and successful, and everything in between. But by the end of that relationship, it's hard to decipher, what and who we hate, and/dislike more. Them, or ourselves. Ever wonder, just for a minute, why others in circle of friends never act(ed) this same way? It has to become an item of interest at some point, right? The answer to each and every successful relationship is the same: They aren't unhappy with themselves, or their spouse. It's usually a direct reflection of themselves.

We're never going to find a relationship amongst us nowadays that is how it's fictitiously displayed in the movies and on television. The obligatory plot twist of "when will he/when will she", then they finally do, and they both live happily ever after. I mean, honestly! I sarcastically blame fairytale cartoons and movie-makers everywhere for filling our heads with unrealistic expectations!

Naturally, once we see a façade of a romantic encounter, and we basically fall in love with the scenario, so much so that we end up wanting that, or a very similar serendipitous encounter to happen to us. Only to have the gravity hit that normalcy is the life we're in. Then, disappointment can set in, because we all want that climatic, emotionally crescendo-ing moment with the man or woman we want to fall in love with, or hope that they fall in love with us. Reality truly does "bite".

Most relationships end because they weren't right for each other anyways, but they wanted to give it an honest shot, so they threw caution into the wind, and tried, and then subsequently failed. Hat's off to them otherwise for having the guts and gumption to do what 60-70% of other couples can't, or are otherwise incapable of doing and committing. Then, over half of those that *do* commit to marriage get divorced anyway, and I know what most if not all that are reading these words may feel that I am just another "marriage cynic". I'm not. And I'll prove it. Experience in this and other marital, and divorced realms qualifies me to take a unique stance on this very subject. It is this: Love is so much of the "little things". It's the casual and occasional touches, the flirts, the boxes of chocolates, the trinkets, and the love notes and the sonnets and poems exchanged. It's also even more than that! Because the hopeless romantic that's crammed inside of my apparent scarred psyche still totally embraces the fact that it's real. I do, in fact believe in it. In love.

At the end of the day, those couples that are truly right for each other, still in fact will endure through all the same tests, trials, triumphs, failures and disappointment that the rest of us all have to go through. The biggest difference is, they simply don't let it tear them apart, *or* let any circumstance take them down. It alters and changes from time to time, situation by situation, but these same couples, these same marital stalwarts all share another critical component and attitude to their successful marriage. It is this: no matter what, and no matter where, one of those persons will stand up and fight for that relationship and marriage no matter what, and no matter the score. If it's the right thing to pursue, and they have a little (okay, a lot) of luck smile down upon them, they'll see that moment for what it really is. That moment that if they flinch in the wrong and/or right direction, could change everything. Then, they constantly choose their marriage, their love and their relationship over their pride.

So what if it didn't work out the way we planned? What if the counterpart in the marriage/relationship doesn't "do their part" and will not, and does not fight for the marriage in return? I actually address this topic more thoroughly in another chapter later in this book titled: "How To Know When To Get Out". You're welcome to skip ahead, but this next segment is a slightly different direction, with a darker twist. It's almost too unbelievable to sit across the table at one's spouse/loved one, and listen to all the excuses as to why they don't want to be married to us anymore. I use the term "excuses" because that's exactly what they are. Shallow, hollow reason(s) for their comprehensive selfishness to bail on a relationship that they could have (and might I add should have) otherwise saved, if they just would have put in the same, if not slightly less effort and time to choose, and keep choosing to love and work on the marriage. Agency is so infinitely powerful that it basically requires all of us to respect and accept the actions of others, even if those actions are severely detrimental to the relationship. We just don't have to *agree* with their poor decision(s). I use the term "accept" not in the approval context. That conflicts with my next-to-last sentence that addresses the "respect and accept" concepts. I am referring to the context in which "accept" refers to the opposite reaction and emotion for "denial". Denial is a tool and a device of the Adversary. Acceptance is the antithesis of denial. Ergo why it's so very important to embrace the "acceptance" of others and their poor decisions. There should be some form of vindication, some self-contrived release knowing that these decisions that our significant other has executed will not ultimately affect us. It's simply not the case, unfortunately. It's a direct effect on us and our children (if the case calls for it) and usually for the worse. Granted, divorce allows for the two persons to now co-exist in an otherwise very uninhabitable situation. But the complication only gets worse. There are custody battles that have lasted for years. There's the moderation of property. There's visitation differential. There are the out-of-state contingencies to consider. There's summer, and school time visitation to consider. This is only the beginning. Why do I disclose all of this? Hopefully it works out that any one of you that are reading this decides against pursuing a divorce. Hopefully the aftermath of the strenuous legal process lessens your resolve to move forward to getting a divorce. Then, there's the other side of that coin. Hopefully if there's those of you still hell-bent on getting a divorce, that you're able to commit to it, and see it through to the bitter, ugly, horrific and maniacal end. Because you will very likely pass through every-last-one of those diabolical adjectives. In some cases, a few times over. I won't tell you that divorce is easy, seamless, or even simple.

It's not. I am confident that those of you reading this would largely agree that it's quite possible the most difficult, strenuous, and impossible thing you've ever had to endure. In the same breath, it wouldn't be so easy, if it wasn't so *worth* it. This is still is, and will remain a very subjective statement.

A Day in the Dating Life

We've all been there. We meet someone, it goes well. Too well. Like we've been missing each other's friendship all along and the "why couldn't we have met *them* sooner" feeling. So we go with it. Trying to maintain, to keep it together, all the while edging closer to that feeling and/or that level of "kinda crazy about him/her". Then the constant internal struggle of "Am I feeling too much too soon? What if they don't feel the same? What if *they* like me more than I like them? What if this whole thing is just like the last 75 pseudo-relationships that I've both talked myself into, and then consequently out of? While simultaneously reliving the same excitement and then disappointing heartbreak of the previous 75-pseudo-relationships, all for the sake of wanting to *have* someone special in my life again? Is it, and are they worth the risk of yet another heartbreak? Then, reality galvanizes your frame. You gently realize that you're "just doing it again" that you're over thinking it, and they really don't have such crazy feelings for you, and now you're back to being less crazy, bordering on level-headed. Your pulse decelerates, and your pupils contract from prior dilation. You sweep your emotions aside, and then you begin to take stock of your emotional status quo. Then, bam! The shine is off the proverbial apple. That adorable little girl, or enchanting boy that you once were kind of going crazy over, isn't who the represented themselves to be. They flip a 180-degree emotional U-Turn, and now, they're the person that uses your dignity as a trash bag liner to clean up any shreds of sanity that might be left over in the emotional dumpster fire of one's heart.

Ironic, doesn't it seem that relationships don't quite work out the way we see them turnout in the movies and TV. That's the most obvious of illusions, right there. The never-ending going back and forth, back and forth, "will he say this to her" and "will she respond? Will it be the way our happy little ending needs to in order to further perpetuate the illusion? That illusion that the "exception to the rule" is in fact, the norm, when in fact, all things considered, the norm is still the rule, but that consistent lie isn't how Hollywood makes their cheddar." Long diatribe, I'm aware. So the movie-scene couple in this hypothetical finally *does* say and do what the script says they will, and it miraculously falls into place. Then the cue for "happily ever after" is called in. Give me a break. Call me a skeptic, but the over-romanticizing of relationships and falling in love is hype. It is. Why? Because these movies never tell show what happens *after* the Hollywood-style courtship. So many relationships end anyway because one person deems that they weren't right for each other to start with, (shouldn't the *other* person at least have some sort of say in that "decision"? You'd think!) and statistically, *half* the marriages end in divorce anyway, with an ever-increasing list of casualties. You may start thinking that I'm just another male drone with a keyboard barking at the notion that happiness is the grand illusion. Don't be so quick to jump to said conclusion about me. There's *always* a method to my verbal madness. I'm not the cynic some may take me for. Here's why: It just so happens that I *do* believe that love is, and forever will be about the little things you/we do for each other. Guys, we still need to move the chocolate-covered strawberries in the direction of our ladies. Ladies you still need to let your man feel like he's king of the castle, and that he's the guardian of your world. See, along with men instinctively needing to be the "hunter/gatherer" we need that validation from our women. When we don't feel wanted, accepted, manly, and that we've let you down in those critical areas, we can quickly lose sight of who we are, and who we are/were to you as your man. When that happens, it's easy to give up and stop the much-needed pursuit of your love and acceptance. We can then demonstrate a certain weakness that comes as a result of our current insecurity, a propensity to seek out and find that same validation, and acceptance from someone else that freely bestows our otherwise lost manhood.

Men, we're guilty of this same pattern of behavior too! Our women need our love even more so! Now, those couples that are truly right for each other will endure through the same trials, troubles, struggles, temptations, etc., that everyone else goes through. The biggest difference is, they don't let it tear apart their relationship. Either one of those people will at different times and for different reasons take a stand and fight for their relationship diligently, without fail. Someone will do, or say something that will demonstrate to the other person that "HEY! *You're worth fighting for. WE'RE worth fighting for. Forever.*

Do we think, in an effort to avoid all the mundane nuances of dating and courtship that we are just friends first, before we invest in any form of an emotionally serious relationship? Those of us that are lucky enough to start a relationship as friends, or with the willingness to learn more about each other on a friend basis but with the underlying intent of a romantic interest. This can be, theoretically, the wisest way to go about our relationships especially with prospective marital and eternal partner in mind. I mean consider the alternative: you never hear of people saying "He/She was my best lover, or make out, etc., so that's why I married them!" You almost always hear: "He/She was my best friend, the have seen me at my worst and see me at my best, and still loves me through all of it!" Yes. That's often how the story goes. It's true that we need to have some romantic interest and physical attraction in order to want to pursue a friendship and obvious romantic relationship. But the romance and the physical aspect of relationship should never interfere with developing the friendship side of things. In fact it's almost always preceding the romantic and physical development in a relationship. Now I'm not going to fool you into thinking that I've always followed this pattern. I unfortunately have burned many bridges and affected once gracious friendship and relationships by going about this process all wrong. This is one of the reasons why I have chosen to write such a book is to have others learn from my mistakes. If there's one thing that I can give to divorced persons and serial daters, and the perpetually single individuals, it is this: we need to stop wasting time trying to find the perfect person, and focus a significant portion of our efforts in all of our efforts on *being* the right person. Once we are the right person, the Lord will put the right person in our path, spirit will communicate to us, and without knowing who what when where or why, we will just *know*. How do I know? Because the Lord will not let us down in the most important decision we have to make! The great thing about putting our trust in the Lord, and doing our part, is once we have done our part, not only does He make up the rest, but He has made ample provisions for us.

The Dating List

One of the primary struggles single persons nowadays face that wasn't too prevalent, if at all in the earlier stages of dating is criteria. Most, if not everyone, wants their partner to be perfect or, their partner to save them from their current situation, is as unrealistic and unfair of an expectation to put on an imperfect person, which all of us are. So when we go about our way acting a fool, we fail to let others be imperfect, and relationships dwindle by a thread or have already snapped. An even more difficult factor is to let our partners be imperfect despite us being aware of all of our own imperfections. We feel it's appropriate for our partners to give *us* allowances to be imperfect. As if they're the ones that need to have their standards higher or morals higher or even worse, make them responsible for our safety and salvation. That is just simply unfair and unrealistic! Our partners are not supposed to be, nor are they ever going to be our saviors! Sometimes our greatest strengths can consequently be our greatest weaknesses. For instance, someone with the wonderful childlike and playful nature might also be impulsive and immature. Someone who has an intense way of thinking about things might not adjust on the logical aspect to avoid the mess of emotional disruption. These false expectations utterly put a damper on our own expectations and can corrupt our overall position for dating somebody, but we turn was should be an enjoyable experience of dating a term I like to call "investi-dating".

It's true, that's dating should be an enjoyable and exciting experience. Just like anything else that comes of age and experience, we find ourselves in a rut. This knowledge and wisdom and experience plays a bigger role of a disadvantage than we had ever hoped. The "innocence of youth" is lost on us grown adults! Terms like "jaded", "experienced", "cynical", and "exhausted" can, for the most part, plague our thoughts, which impacts our words, which also further impacts our actions, which ultimately has a resolute and unyielding effect on our destiny. Which, I totally get, as each one of us that are single and looking for a partner, has faced an innumerable amount of heartache, disappointments, surrender, sacrifice, emotional endurance, perspective widening and narrowing. Honestly there are just too many adjectives and too many scenarios to really give proper representation too. So, suffice it to say, that despite the fact that dating is a necessary evil, and everyone has different ways techniques and tactics and executions of how they date, doesn't always match up with the persons are interested in and eventually the person they're going to end up marrying. Which is even more annoying to those that are subject to enduring "investi-dating". Sure, it may be fun to talk about to those interested parties of family friends and close relatives that, even on the surface, seem like they might care, but ultimately, we find ourselves wanting to be in their position. We may want to have a whole family again, if we were previously married, and wanting to have someone to hold, and someone to belong to. Because that's all anyone wants, right? Be, and to feel loved? To share life's celebrations and downfalls, and disappointments, and highlights. Sounds reasonable enough to me. So we further embark on "investi-dating". I know the times that I personally have been guilty of this tactic, I find myself getting into the doldrums of going through the motions, which, if the other person's really paying attention, can be vaguely insulting. But it's the same old story. We're the ones that are supposed to be given and made the exceptions, while everyone else around us has to follow the rules? Sure seems that way sometimes. It's not supposed to be fair; I would love to know where it is written that life is fair, especially when it comes to dating. So, I'd like to dig deeper and find out why it is that we are so quick to investigate somebody on a superficial level, than it is for us to open our hearts and learn to love. Then give a portion of our love to that person - if even on a friendly basis, to see if we might respond to growth somewhere. Or, better yet, to see how they respond to our ingenuousness towards them. Love, compassion, ingenuity and overall embracing the inhuman ability to divinely love someone and the mere execution of this act will always be the answer. It always be the best dating practice.

Introspection

As a single guy, I have never personally felt any extraordinary pressure to find someone, and marry someone with any real urgency. Small confession time, I'm actually quite terrified to bring any girls that I may be dating and have them come meet my family. My reason for my fear is actually pretty simple, and for most of us very understandable. For the most part I am emotionally and mentally above what anyone else in the world really thinks of me or about me. I've been through enough hardships and trials to block out the world's judgments against me, and just live my life happy enough that I can smile at the man in the mirror. I can say my prayers at night holding myself accountable to Heavenly Father, knowing full well there are days that I have struggled mightily, personal issues spiritual issues, sins, shortcomings, and transparently, ungodliness. For the most part I can say that without any reservation for anyone's reaction. But for whatever reason, when it comes to my family, I fear greatly what their thoughts are when I bring a woman over to my house to meet them whether be a simple Sunday family dinner, or a holiday event where significant other would be socially appropriate. I respond this way because I'd like to think that inside each of their heads, they're asking themselves: "Oh, so *this* is your latest 'future travesty'... When are you going to pour the gasoline on this proverbial dumpster fire?" In short, I sincerely feel that my family questions a lot of my romantic decision-making abilities. It's no exception in relationships too. It's not like they look down on me or anything, I just don't have a great track record keeping and maintaining relationships, especially then it comes to the serious levels of marriage. Do I feel judged? Absolutely. Where I am different than most others is that despite the fact that I feel I'm being judged by family friends and relatives, their judgments don't define me. Not one bit. Allowing others judgments against us to affect who we are for a negative, is a strong sign of victim mentality. I simply won't let myself be or demonstrate victim mentality. Which is why I feel I'm more the exception, than the rule when it comes to my family's attitude towards me still being single, and the judgements I'll get from any girl I bring to meet my family. Now don't get me wrong, my family is great. We all would literally lay down our lives for the other person. I'm lucky and fortunate it hasn't come to that! All joking aside, my family has been pretty great and not pressuring me to get married anytime soon. The problem is for a guy like me and other guys like me, is that there are so many great choices out there! I have met, over the last several years of my being single, some of the most incredible single mothers, and most incredible single women that I have ever met at any point of my life. It's almost as if I want to take the time to get to know as many of these great women as I can, so I have a very thorough investigation, in my "investi-dating" to come to a proper conclusion whom I am most compatible with, in whom I am most likely to live the happiest life with, and give the most to in a marriage relationship. This is also unrealistic goal of mine, there are just too many great women, not enough time, and at the end of the day I end up spending money on too many of what will be other men's wives! Dating needs to be much more judicious, much more diplomatic, much more cerebral and conscientious, then the bad practice of dating any girl you find attractive you know in your mind and in your heart, you men have already thought of two or three women, or in the women's case the men, that you already have in considered a dating pipeline, of ones that you would love to really give an honest shot too. But for whatever reason, reluctance, fear getting heartbroken or just overall inability to trust yourself in making a good decision when it comes to relationships for once. True, there is a lot at stake, but what we really look at ourselves, and the opportunities that are scattered all around us to meet quality people the only bad decision is to not give yourself, and another person an honest shot while the timing is greatest. But take courage? Of course! Do you have to swallow your pride, and be willing to let the miracle happen? Absolutely! Will it take you "going out on a limb?" Most assuredly! But think about the end result: "going out on a limb" is the best choice, because isn't that where of the fruit is? The defense rests. It's considerably disappointing that injustices happen. What makes them even more disappointing is that they most often happen to those who least deserve them. Ergo the appropriateness of the pejorative term "injustice". It's a shame they exist at all. But the reality is that they do. All around us. To the undeserving and the innocent. Shamefully, we all walk around the "walking wounded", and the casualty list grows. If there's any "snow" to be found in this proverbial "dirt storm" is that it's necessary. "Smooth sailing never a skilled sailor made". Or so they say. Make room for trials, Allow for them to happen, embrace them! For when we blow through them, the remaining space where they once existed, now becomes triumph, and pure character.

Bouncing Back

When we are in the throes of divorce, perhaps the last thing we're thinking about is how were going to bounce back from all of this. It's a very daunting prospect, if we give it the proper respect and perspective it deserves. For every person it's going to be different on how to bounce back. Bouncing back is very subjective and certainly on a case-by-case basis. It's one of only two choices we have left once we've hit rock-bottom. Because it's so different for every individual person, there really is no one way to "bounce back" necessarily. But I can certainly point you in the right direction as to how it starts. They say once you've hit rock-bottom, you can only go up after that. I'm not going to debate that, I'm sure I could, but this is an optimistic chapter. Most everything with this sort of movement involves a mental and emotional determination to rise from the dust, so to speak, and build upon and improve upon our current situation. The question is, what exactly is it that you want? How do you want to bounce back? How you going to build your life so that a year, and/or two years down the road those who wanted to see you fail, are unable to laugh at you anymore? For some of us it's going to take a little longer than 1 to 2 years for some of us less. Again, it's a case-by-case basis. Everyone circumstances are and are going to always be different. It also requires us to look inward to see where we want to be. Some people don't have that far to go; some people have monuments to build. So what is it that you want? Write it down. Our mind and our subconscious have a way of creating and/or devising a way to achieve whatever it is that we want, at least uncovering a pathway to that destination. A dream written down with the dates becomes a goal. A goal broken down into steps becomes a plan. A plan backed by action makes our dreams come true. The "immaterial" somehow then becomes "material". It's no longer abstract, now it's tangible. Now it has wheels, now it has traction. Now comes the hard part, once we are filled with resolve to better our lives and better our future, step two is staying focused and staying motivated. The execution of such is never easy, and nor is it supposed to be. Nothing great ever came easy. Nor will it. We'll face opposition, repeatedly, almost relentlessly. A deciphering factor for me that is kept me motivated to achieve several of my goals and dreams is knowing that I have heaven smiling down on me, and the hosts of heaven cheering me on. What is also equally motivating is knowing that there is a dark force out there that would love for me to fail. This same dark force not only wants to see me fail, but wants to see me blame God for my failures and then resent God for not spoon feeding me what needs to be earned and deserved. It's always been confusing to me why people blame God for their hardships and trials and extreme conditions in their life. God is not a vindictive God, insomuch that He is going to cause you to suffer without some sort of way to strengthen you throughout the process. He will not just give us extremely difficult trials troubles tribulations because He wants to be entertained and see how we do. His actions are always righteously motivated, celestially pure and perfect, and most importantly are designed to take us to the next step towards our own exaltation, which He cannot wait to give us! But in the same breath, He *can* wait; He has infinite patience, as a result of His Divine Nature, endless trials and tribulations that He went through once upon a time. Yes, you understand me correctly. Heavenly Father is eagerly waiting to help us bounce back! In the scriptures we read that "men are that they might have joy". We are meant only to experience misery and sorrow and trials and tribulations, never to dwell in them. So, I've asked myself, "what are you waiting for?" Our trials will stand in our way like centurions, and feed our souls and minds countless excuses to prevent any and all progress. Ask yourself again, what *are* you waiting for? Later? It's already "later". This is the worst time to postpone the improvement. These are the last days! We've heard prophecy after prophecy telling us about the perils and the troubles and the commotions that are going to abound in these last days. Procrastinate procrastination! Let's just get the spiritual growing pains over with, so that we can start experiencing a higher form of living that so desperately awaiting us. What you have to lose other than stumbling out of the gate? Which everyone will likely at some point do. Life is awkward enough and sometimes it comes easier for others. As for the rest of us that need a bit of a learning curve, or we simply need something explained to us in a way that only we can understand by our divine Teacher who knows how to portray the message. Elder Neal A. Maxwell once said in the October 2001 General Conference "Though we live in a failing world, we have not been sent here to fail." If you sow your thoughts, you reap your actions. If you sow your actions, you reap your habits. If you sow your habits, you reap your character. If you sow your character, you reap your destiny. We cannot break it down any simpler than that. Don't recall that it's even possible; no one has thrown away their last chance! We can change, repent, and we can come back. A key part to this bouncing back is being humble enough to take suggestions, help, guidance and sound leadership from those looking on who love us and care for us. In fact, in this spiritually broken state of mind that we may find ourselves in climbing out of the dust on away to wanting to bounce back and become more than we ever have been, this just might be the best time for us to take on that sort of emotional responsibility. The best way to repair ourselves and to fill in the gaps is to serve our families, our Heavenly Father's Kingdom, and others in general. Service the rent we pay for membership in God's kingdom. So, don't give up on yourself.

If you're still reading (which I hope you are) You are likely one of those adults that has children as a result of a current or their former marriage. Perhaps you have children just in general. They need your example. The pressure to fail is always high, but it's all about perspective. That's one of the missing facets we find out about ourselves during the triumphant over trials part is that we are often quite the catch! We're slowly overcoming the word. There are a lot of messed up dark experiences that can cloud our heads, but at the same time, it can enable the ability to learn from the past. That will lead us to greener pastures even after our divorce and breakups. There's nothing wrong with thinking we can still have it all amongst the chaos in the white picket fences inside our heart and soul. What if one enables the other, or what if one destroys the other? The temptation is now stronger than ever to hit the "reset" button. We all have moments in our life where we wish we could hit a reset button, and whatever we just experienced could somehow be exchanged for a different outcome. Now that we are made aware of whatever choices that lead up to us wanting to reset our current situation, in hopes to experience a better outcome. As tremendous as this would be to have that ability, one of many problems we can see with this fantasy is that we would now lack the experience and the lessons learned that we should have gained from this reset moment. Even if we could somehow actually reset the situation, we would then lose all of those lessons and knowledge to be gained and important blessings that we wouldn't have otherwise been qualified to receive. The concept of time travel has always been a fantasy of mankind, and it's easy to see how simple that power or privilege or technology would be so ultimately dangerous, especially if it fell into the wrong hands. In light of this concept, if we have ever lived through an experience we want to hit the reset button on, we haven't really learned or embraced the lesson that we were supposed to, as a result of their passing to a certain trial. Now, I realize that not everybody shares that perception. Once trials of any magnitude are met, most everybody seeks help or advice or some assistance in any way the outside of their own home.

As every last one of us deserves love on a physical, emotional, unconditional, and eternal levels. Every last one of us deserves needs to give love and receive those same emotions in return. Oddly enough, unconditionally. Once we've committed to somebody and a mutual love and appreciation is demonstrated often early and actively between these two persons, you can get very greedy and appropriately selfish with your spouse. Compunctions are a tool of the adversary. All a "regret" really is – is a lesson we haven't learned, or sometimes just missed. When you're married, nearly everything is black and white. Who you live with, what you do with that person, when you do it. When you're divorced, that proverbial "black and white" line now becomes "Grey". We cannot attempt to "look up" as it were, to the size and height of the ladder that we have to climb. Doing so can surely cause even a disabling fear to even want to get started *to* climb it. Climbing the ladder is a necessity for our personal growth. It's the way of things. If we just stand and "hang on" to the part of the ladder we currently find ourselves on, neither "growing" (climbing) or digressing (descending) well, we've all heard the old adage "idle hands are the devils work". Fear. It's nothing to really be afraid of. Everything has it's opposite, just like fear can be used for good. Now, hear me out, we can use this as a more of a "means to an end". How, you may ask? Think of a reason you were motivated by fear. What did it cause you to do? How did it cause you to react? How did it cause you to overcome a weakness? How many weaknesses were overcome by acting out of fear? Was the weakness directly affected? That may seem like an unusual line of thinking, but ponder on that. Any fear that we have in our mind or body is a direct result of a weakness we currently may have. We are not afraid of something we have confidence in already, those of us that have the ability to walk are unafraid of letting our motor skills take over and having our knees bend and feet plant on the ground, while we place one foot in front of the other. Those of us that lift weights or exercise and have certain routines we do, simply are not afraid or fear the motions or the exercise routine. Now consider the alternative, fear can be largely based on an uncertainty that we currently have. Something we may be personally may be unfamiliar with or have struggled with and may cause mental blocks to overshadow our confidence. Now, what I mean by having fear as a means to an end, I'm simply stating that fear can be a stepping stone on a progressive staircase as it were, that can and will compel us to perform a certain act for a much better, more glorious cause. For instance, out of respect of a situation or relationship. Admittedly, I was motivated by fear in a number of different occasions in my marriage. What I later discovered is that fear, or being motivated by fear as a corrective gesture to perform certain acts, (and in my case a corrective behavior), would be done so as to appease my spouse at the time. After so long, of performing certain acts out of fear (which fear at the time was derived from fear of hurting or offending my then-wife, or by demonstrating any level of a lack of respect to her or towards her), I found that fear can be a tool to achieve higher understanding of why I really should be motivated to perform certain acts out of respect and or love. Who would have thought, acting out of fear would lead to love! Whether it be working on keeping the house clean while she was away so when she came into the door she had a nice clean home to open the door to. Taking the lead on picking up the dinner plates and the currently dirty dishes from the meal preparation, and taking them over to the sink to be washed in the dishwasher. The truth is, fear *is* good. It can, if used as a healthy tool, keep you from being a bad spouse, and a bad person. The trick is, you can't let it paralyze you. Like we said earlier, everything has its opposite. As fear is such a pejorative term, the way we try to use fear as an ally to motivate us to higher ground and to a better understanding of things. It can disable our spirit and motivation and even our mind, if we let it. So now the question becomes, how do we prevent fear from paralyzing us? I offer three suggestions:

1) Always remember that fear is one of the best tools the adversary knows how to use against us. And as a result of that tool of fear, let's be clear on what a tool is used for. It is used to manipulate an inanimate object. In this example, this tool will remain the concept of fear. Our hearts, minds, spirits, and motivation are the metaphorical inanimate objects. Often times, the tool of fear is already wedged into our hearts mind spirits and motivation, and the adversary's just waiting for the right opportunity to turn the tool to his advantage. Make no mistake; this will never be turned to *our* advantage if it's in the adversary's hands. As we all are clarion aware, everything the adversary does is to destroy, disintegrate, decimate, and distort our path and understanding of how to achieve eternal life. Keeping that in mind, our agency can be his strength to how far *we allow him* to manipulate all of his inanimate objects he has in his arsenal of tools. The more correct decisions we make with our

agency, the less strength he has to manipulate his tools against us. Contrastingly, the poorer decisions we make and the more we fall into his temptations, the more power and the more turns he gets stronger his influence and has power is over us to further weaken our resistance to his evils.

2) Strengthening our agency and our character against his want for our spiritual paralysis. This is done, by making countless correct decisions which enable us to develop protective spiritual manners. Fortunately for us, there are so many devices strengths and opportunities for us to strengthen our resistance that only to the influence of the adversary, but to build overall character that will draw us closer to our Heavenly Father, through the atonement of Jesus Christ.

3) Finally, coming to grips with our weaknesses, recognizing them, embracing them, as we read in Ether 12:24 we are "given weaknesses so that we may become humble" if we approach the Savior with our acknowledged weaknesses (this doesn't have to be a comprehensive acknowledgement of all of our weaknesses, just the ones we feel best prepared to tackle now) and then placing these weaknesses before Him, kneeling in prayer asking Him to guide us and our patience with ourselves, that current weaknesses will become our strengths. Sometimes this happens without us even bringing our weaknesses to the Savior, I know many weaknesses I used to have that I no longer have similar because I was able to work on them, but they are brought to my attention so glaringly obvious that they needed to be addressed immediately. The Savior aided my progression regardless. He blesses those who take action with righteousness as the endgame. Most definitely at certain points I did approach the Savior asking for mercy from Him and patience with myself as He and I tackled these weaknesses, together. See, there's more to all of this that we mere mortals perhaps want to acknowledge and recognize. We have a loving Heavenly Father and the limitless source of spiritual strength encouragement and love from the Savior who not only died for us, but currently, and will forever live for us as well, if we simply ask Him. I'm sure he's proud of us to an extent once He sees us tackle a problem all by ourselves. But in the end, especially with us working through these fears and dancing with the devil in the meantime, wouldn't we be eternally better served if we forget that we are not left to our own devices, and clasp that Divine reach that, as Isaiah states of "…His hand is stretched out still." (Isaiah 9:17).

Forgiveness

This is going to be one of the most difficult chapters to write. Forgiveness, especially at the magnitude of breaking up ones family over selfish impulses and desires and actions, seems almost impossible at first. But that can be (among many other reasons) because the victim almost masochistically chooses to hold the offender in such contempt, that forgiveness can become viewed as a weakness to the victim. I think it's fair enough to say that victims will view the actual act of forgiving their offender as a luxury, and a charitable act that the offender absolutely does not deserve! What may be difficult to see is that the adversary is literally playing both sides of this proverbial "coin" as it were. Not only did he contrive, tempt, execute, and then consequently win the battle of ours and our offenders agency, but now that the offense was executed, the offender can be drawing further and further away from the Lord (subjective to the severity of the offense) but now that the victim is in an emotionally vulnerable situation, the adversary will then fill the victims heads of revenge, self-loathing, manipulations, depressions, and alienation. Sure there may be some other adjectives, but work with me here. For myself and others, the forgiveness process is not only lengthy, but it's so easy to approach forgiveness with a gripping sense of reluctance. See, most of us can understand that forgiveness is a voluntary mercy that the offender for all intents and purposes, may not initially deserve. The adversary tried to trick me into thinking that forgiveness is not only a way of showing weakness, but even worse it strengthens and enables my own pride to the point I can slowly convince myself that not only did I have the right to be angry with my offender, I also had the right to exact terrible revenge. The Lord has told us for centuries that vengeance is His, and it is. Some may ask and even wonder why that is. My personal response to that same question is that God has total and complete love for both parties both the offender and the victim, and is able to impartially judge both parties as well. He has the ultimate understanding and luxury of knowing to what extent the offense has caused, and also the inherent damage at the victim has incurred. He also knows both parties full stories. He knows to the fullest extent the cause-and-effect of factors I may not have fully considered. Combined with his total omniscience, God also approaches any and all situations with a perfect and fearless love for every person involved. An attribute, and a frame of mind, us mere mortals simply cannot fully execute, or properly judge, nor take into consideration all parties involved and maintain a level of perfect understanding. It simply isn't in us. As a mere mortal, I'm too far removed from the Divine Nature of our Heavenly Father in my mortal, fallen estate to really fully execute perfect vengeance with the Lords ability for total love. We all know mercy cannot rob justice, no more than justice should consider the opportunity for mercy. As most every case involving mercy and justice is not only circumstantial, but perhaps more importantly, is on such a case-by-case basis, that it's rare to find two circumstances that they are so much the same. They can allow for that all too rare allowance of a cookie-cutter approach solution. Luckily, we needn't burden our temporal-versioned perspective with vengeance because we're so prone to overreact anyway that any attempt at vengeance is best suited for the Lord anyway. I never knew how strong I am and was until I forgave someone that may not ever be sorry. Nor feel like they were in the wrong to begin with, until I accept the apology I'll essentially never get. Forgiveness is very similar to freedom. In that one begets the other when it comes to offenses both given, and taken. Embrace forgiveness. I had to trust the Savior on this. It won't be easy. In fact, it will be hard, nigh impossible. But the way I crave freedom, if I want to live life without hate and malice, and contempt for some other person, then I got to let it go. There are so many active clichés about forgiveness, and moving on that the persistent rhetoric of them is nearly condescending to the all-too-familiar crowd that is everyone else. For instance: "Holding a grudge is the same as the victim drinking poison, and hoping that the offender feels the effects." If we possess no forgiveness in our hearts, then living is even a worse punishment than death will ever be. In fact, forgiveness, and the early development of that divine attribute is a beautiful defense against future offenses. It's like protective, spiritual and emotional Teflon! If we can condition our character to be quick to forgive, and become more understanding and empathetic of others, especially our offenders, then we're allowing, enabling, activating more and peace, and Divine happiness in ourselves. Arguably one of the most difficult components to forgiveness is arriving at an emotional and mental disposition where we're tired of the hate, where we're tired of the pollution hate creates in our soul. The adversary is so good and so crafty at disguising his diabolical products in our souls that he can make hatred, malcontent, (you name it) and the worst of his damning arsenal appeal to our spiritual sensitivities. He can disguise it so it's even a borderline pleasurable experience! Any of us who have ever disliked someone or something to the extent that we loved to dislike them or it, is a perfect example of this poisonous act! Those of us that continue on in entertaining and even embracing those diabolical activities slowly and unknowingly give the adversary, the enemy of our souls, more control over our agency. This desensitizing process is designed for one thing, and one thing only, to slowly draw us further and further away from the light, and safety of our Heavenly Father, and His Kingdom. To prove that last statement, consider the awful disposition the adversary pursues for us: "That all men might be miserable like unto himself." (2Nephi 2:27). Forgiveness, as it would seem, is never easy. I'm personally inclined to believe that any act or endeavor to pull away from our natural man tendencies is ever going to be "easy". Of course, that's a very subjective statement. Which hinges largely upon our own personal relationship (if it can be called such) with our natural man tendencies. And, of which, I'll even dare to venture the opinion, our own "Anti-self", as I had suggested in a former chapter. It wouldn't surprise me if our own "Anti-self's" are not only synonymous with the natural man, but one of the same! So some of you may be asking yourselves at this point, "how do we weaken the adversaries 'grip' on us and draw closer to Christ?" The late Elder Neal A. Maxwell states it perfectly: "One of the best ways to put off the natural man is to starve him. Weakened, he is more easily dislodged, otherwise he insists on getting his ticket punched on every stop on the train!" (The Seventh Commandment, A Shield" Oct. 2001 General Conference) Let's dissect that statement for a second, shall we? Elder Maxwell suggests that we "starve the natural man" in this very effective metaphor, starving simply suggests that we engage in activities and commit acts of service that are alternatively contrary to natural man tendencies. Attending church services regularly, sincerely repenting for even minor sins and disobedience, finding ways to both love and serve our neighbors in even the most minor especially the most major of circumstances, and, if when a position to do so, regular temple attendance. Now, it doesn't stop there, the list of things we can do to "starve" the natural man, is just about as endless as the eternities themselves. It occurs to me that the choice is simple. We use our agency to develop protective spiritual manners, which in the development of such, strengthens and reinforces our spiritual character so that we can eventually possess the character to which any temptation never really registers in our mind. We will "have no more disposition to do evil, but do good continually" (Mosiah 5:2). Or, we can allow ourselves to become complacent in our discipleship, go about our commandments and covenants casually, really only fulfilling them when it's convenient for us. We may find ourselves justifying a little sin here, allowing a little lewd behavior there, all while underestimating the enemy of our souls allowing him more and more power over our agency and choices. This slow, and barely noticeable painful process is one of the adversary's best tactics to witness this desensitizing, distorting process: "and thus the devil cheateth their souls, and leadeth them away carefully down to hell." (2Nephi 28:21) Justification, and rationalization, are two of the adversary's most popular weapons in his vast arsenal of soul-destroying execution. That we have further examined with some strong emphasis on the consequences of allowing the adversary to attack our ability, or inability to forgive someone, or anyone, it's far better for us to see this with a 30,000 foot aerial view, than to be living it. This is one of the many reasons why forgiveness is so critical! Still to this day, one scripture that will always blow my mind on the profound value of forgiveness and how quick the Christ was able to forgive his murderous parties despite their wicked determination to take his life, (and their eventual succession of it) that even while on the cross, enduring arguably the worst pain a human has ever endured, he was somehow able to utter the words "Father, forgive them, for they know not what they do." (Luke 23:34) I currently do not possess that level or ability of forgiveness. This example tells me how much further I have to go. Alternatively, I do not and cannot let the length of the journey to become like Christ discourage me, or shut my motivation down from this path. Because I want it. I always have, and I always will. I do not have the audacity to write words on these pages and have you the reader even for a moment, believe that I have all the answers to forgiveness for that I have forgiven everyone that has ever crossed me in any way. I still have more than enough persons that I need to forgive. These feelings and impressions that I am wordsmithing, are the sum of a grand total of not only lessons I have learned, lessons I still learning. They are part of a larger, grander scheme equaling the totality of the formula for forgiveness, and the ultimate achieving of total forgiveness. There moments that I personally struggle, provoke or otherwise engage, with persons directly involving my divorce. It used to be a lofty, almost unachievable goal to forgive someone or persons that had such an impact on the breaking apart of my family. That may sound like a very pejorative statement, it's a concept that married people may never understand, and unhappily married people are tempted to "dip their toe" into. That concept of breaking apart your family, so that you and your estranged spouse can go on living your lives independent from each other, completely separate and apart from the path that led you to be together, kills a part of you. Anyone who's unfamiliar with having forks in your road both personally, professionally, and on a familial level, clearly hasn't lived life outside of a fairytale or cartoon. Or they are just plain old ignorant, and/or in denial. This act of emotional murder, or perhaps a better term would be emotional suicide or sabotage, may not be such a bad thing. I have found this as a tool to use in difficult and even very difficult situations. I use this as a shield, as it were to block the haunting, and numbing sensations that are the result of the aftermath of the perpetual broken hearts, disappointments, discouragements, and what largely seems like the day-to-day make up of life as we may know it in this fallen sphere. Now, that's not to say that I don't feel any of those symptoms, I certainly do from time to time, but what this trial-turned-blessing has aided me to do is to not only feel less of those symptoms, but the ability to get over them a lot quicker than the average person. I'm positive I'm not the only one that has this ability. Sure, there are lots of us that have gone through similar feelings and symptoms have embraced this incredibly valuable tool to get over, and be done with the emotional side of the hurt, pain, and suffering. Collectively, when trials, troubles, disappointments, and heartache, come at us, and they inevitably, will, we have a choice. We can either use them as stepping stones to elevate our spirits and strengthen them against future trials, or we can fall victim to the adversary and stumble over them. The adversary will want us to keep stumbling until we ultimately fall and collapse spiritually. It almost always boils down to choice. Our choosing how to face, confront, and overcome trials. In conclusion of this chapter on forgiveness, when these trials, troubles, and tribulations bombard us, we also have to learn to not only be patient with ourselves, but to learn how to forgive ourselves! We can either be our own best friend, or our own worst enemy. Those of us that have ever been our own worst enemy, seem to have this unfailing knack of self-loathing, and getting in our own way. It almost seems as if we are deliberately being *given* the right thing to do, with the right guidance and instructions from on high, we may even recognize the good choice. But we intentionally choose the wrong choice almost in an effort to receive the wrong kind of attention the whole self-defeatist type attitude and persona. I maintain we become our own best friend! I want nothing more than to see my success and experience it, and live it, and share with others especially my daughters. Nothing makes me happier than to see my daughter's faces when they see daddy succeeding! We have all the tools, we have the necessary means, wherewithal, even the integrity. So why not take up our own arms, be nicer to ourselves, *forgive ourselves* once in a while, and be supportive and its strength to our own cause?! No one else is going to fight for us, so we might as will fight for ourselves. Oh, and one more thing. There are many things I enjoy and love about writing, I love watching a sentence come together, the composition of the thoughts in my head, and watching the feelings and emotions appear on the page. In essence, the living manifestation of "bleeding on the page" as it were. It's moments like composing this chapter, where I have a renewed afresh perspective and appreciation for the principle of forgiveness. I have learned so much from forgiveness, and how to apply it at this point in my life than any time before. What I shared can merely be a foundation, building on a theory in so many words, of ways to begin our own forgiveness processes with those who have hurt us or offended us on some of the deepest emotional levels. I just hope that I have contributed in some way to not only the forgiveness process of your own, but the natural byproduct of forgiveness, which is a magnificent fruit of the atonement, and that is peace of mind, piece of body, and peace of heart. The consummate totality of the word "peace".

The Strength Chapter

Strength is such a subjective word. Strength in what exactly? What is strength? If you want to look at it semantically, it can be understood as an area where an individual can be, or is more affluent in comparison to something or someone else. Strength can also come as a result of resistance to an opposing factor as weightlifting is to gravity. As we all know, strengths are a good thing. Using, and playing to our strengths helps us, drives us, and encourages us to continue being good people, or least good at what our strengths are. When the thought of losing my family was beginning to register in my mind, I was mortified, terrified, scared beyond reason, and very, very afraid. I had this debilitating, and paralyzing fear locked inside of my soul that the worst possible things that can happen in life are about to happen to me. I was doomed. Forever to be alienated and ostracized by the otherwise faithful Christian public. I wasn't totally confident with my ability to adapt to such a high stress situation. I felt totally unprepared, and ill-equipped and was all but ready to prepare to sink to the bottom of my depression and misery knowing that on the other side of my then marriage my counterpart had a tremendous advantage because to family members have been involved in divorces and so they would know all of the tricks, all of the manipulations, all of the tactics, and worst of all the ability to legally cripple me, with me being none the wiser.

It's these moments of weakness these glaring moments of patronizing legal hoops to jump through, that a lot of us find our weaknesses. Parenthetically, as if we didn't need more adversity, and exposure of our inherent weaknesses, that can bring us down to a depth and level of the gravity of our situation in a mortifyingly humble stroke of fate. See, we cannot develop strengths if we don't know, or recognize that we have weaknesses. It starts with us at the earliest of ages growing from an infant to a toddler learning how to scoot, crawl, walk, run, until we are fully autonomous in our personal movements and motor skills. Sometimes, and I even dared to venture the opinion that often times we don't know we have weaknesses because we often don't view them as such. They could be simply an area of our life that we have never really explored potential in. I'm I never knew I was going to be so naturally gifted in athletics until I tried shooting a basketball, or swinging a baseball bat or catching a ball. It's not until I threw a football, or strapped a snowboard to my feet, that I learned I had potential to develop these sports. Once we find we have strengths, we get a sense of accomplishment, it's actually quite intrinsic. When the strengths are discovered, and often used in exercise, as we all know we can strengthen them even more so. Even to the point where we can take them on a professional level. I'm building these examples together for a reason. That's one of the beautiful things about writing is seeing the big picture in your mind of how you want this topic or chapter or even paragraph to unfold, and closing your eyes but for a moment, and use the words in your mind to describe every pertinent and necessary detail of this picture in your mind. All of this has led to this verbal crescendo. The Lord has an interesting way of making our strengths become a source of healthy pride, and in the same breath, a way to knock us off our high horses, humble us, and bring us back down to earth. The problem we may face with that is we can blame God and trying to find fault in His methods, which is never fruitful. It is the most unreasonable, and ridiculous gesture for us mere mortals to get mad at God for anything he does. If we believe God and we believe in him, then my argument is fully ratified with the scripture in Moses chapter 1 verse 39 when God says that his work in his glory is to bring to pass the mortality and eternal life of men. He isn't going to do anything that's not going to bless *us,* or work towards our own exaltation. Best of all, He wants us to draw closer to Him. What does this all have to do with strengths? Strengths can lead to confidence, confidence can lead to pride. Pride, if used the wrong way can give us feelings of self-assurance that any change for the better, or a strength we have developed is the cause of our own doing, and has nothing to do with the God that gives us anything that is good, and/or that can be used for good. Elder Henry B. Eyring once said "Pride creates a noise within us that makes the tender voice of the Spirit hard to hear... Soon in our vanity we no longer even listen for it, we can come quickly to think we don't need [the Spirit]. ("Prayer" Oct. 2001 LDS General Conference). I've examined this in my life too many times to know that there is a little bit of ego involved in my strength. These can destroy us. As I've mentioned in other chapters and observations the adversary has his opposite in everything that God has created. He has counterfeited everything the Lord has created. With confidence the opposite of that is devilish pride. It is strictly designed to draw us away from Heavenly Father and rely too much not only our own abilities, but to the point where we feel we don't need or want anything more to do with our Heavenly Father. We want to feed our egos. We want to feel and be impervious to weakness. We want to be, and even exude the façade of being bulletproof. When we have those moments where we exemplify and demonstrate anything less than being bulletproof, who we are, and our true nature and our current character "status quo" is revealed. For better, or for worse. Who will we be? Are we going to be the "Laman and Lemuel" type where you feel shortchanged because of your age, experience, birthright or family rank? Or are you going to remember the source of all your blessings, source of all your strengths throughout every trial and challenge and temptation, and recognize, and renew afresh in whom you trusted? Because I'll tell you one thing, if we rely too heavily on ourselves, or if we rely too heavily upon the arms of flesh (not us or Heavenly Father), the devil doesn't support his children at the last day. He cannot wait for us to feel like we're so self-sufficient, and sell self-dependent, without acknowledging the source of our blessings and self-sufficiency. When that when that moment comes, (and he's waiting for it, mind you) he will not hesitate to leave us there in the dust. Embarrassed, humiliated, alienated, left alone for the rest of the world to point laugh and make a mock of. How many celebrities and others of us have we seen brought to the pinnacle of their careers, and with a few moments of misfortune, bad timing, just enough overindulgence, They lose it all. The adversary having orchestrated the entire thing. The glamour, the glitz, the flashing yet fading lights of stardom, the adversary has made quite a dark living for himself feasting on the souls and our worldly tendencies that Hollywood has indulged on for centuries. Now, don't get me wrong, it isn't just celebrities and the stars that fall. All of us are moments away from the same twist of fate. I've seen this happen to the best people I know that have no fortune at all. They don't even deserve their misfortune, but then again who does? Life is never fair, nor will it be. There's no use trying to escape that truth. One day all of us will have to stop running away from, or trying to outsmart the truth, and let it have its day. Where strength of character, morality, strength of mind, and strength of spirit applies, its byproduct counters all of this mess. Proper application of spiritual strength relying upon the one being who will always, and eternally be strong, and is waiting to give us His same strength-will never fail us. That despite our trials, troubles, disappointments, and failures, as Isaiah puts beautifully and poetically, his hand is stretched out still.

It is the hand of Him, who desires to give *us* everything He has. To which I add: including His immortal and eternal strength.

Going through a divorce and/or a breakup provides us with so many distractions. Some of these distractions are helpful for our personal growth and spiritual maturity because we focus less on the pain we are enduring, and the pain we are witnessing others go through. While we're focusing on licking our own wounds, so to speak, and recovering from emotional and possibly psychological disarray. Contrastingly, one of these distractions is getting caught up and/or spending too much time focusing on less than top priority issues. An example of what I speak of is the concept of prioritizing our decisions. Although I still maintain nothing can really prepare you for going through an enduring your own individual divorce. As no two situations are identical but should be approached as a case-by-case basis, the answer to each is the same. Learning how to adapt to the hand fate deals us. Now I know there are some of you that don't believe in fate, and that's fine. Perhaps a more appropriate term for those is "outcome". While I will choose to continue to use the word fate, those disbelieving in that term may substitute with the word "outcome", or whatever term you believe in. What makes fate and/or outcome such a mesmeric experience is that it is usually the natural end result of an event. Why we are in control of our fate is based on the decisions we make in the process that equals the sum of the combination of our decisions subtracted or added to circumstances and the consequences that occur as a result of our decisions. We are in more control than we realize, especially when it comes to our divorce and breakups. While I referenced the term "distraction" in the previous paragraph, one of the best distractions out there is being more aware. As the cluster of outcomes that metaphorically may appear to be puzzle pieces, that fit together to create some grand emotional "jigsaw puzzle". We can put blinders on and focus only on the puzzle pieces and where they fit. As opposed to taking a step back and seeing the grand landscape and the intending design of the overall jigsaw puzzle. Perspective will always and forever be one of the most powerful and provocative elements in shaping our decisions, and consequently our actions. The problem that becomes focusing more on the puzzle pieces and where they fit is that we can neglect our own personal issues, problems and hang-ups. We may sometimes allow the more important time-consuming and time sensitive issues to pass us by, until ultimately fate takes that decision out of our hands. We are forced with an end results didn't want, or is not the best endgame for our set of circumstances.

Some of the reasons why we stall in making all these decisions is because we're afraid to make the decision for fear that will end up with the results that we not only didn't anticipate, but affects too many people that we want to be accountable for. It's the same old story that every decision and every choice, and a reaction has a consequence. It can also have a reaction to our decision. While the water roils beneath our feet as our ship is slowly sinking, ultimately, fate will have its day. As if we were compelled by fate, we lose the ability to determine the outcome of our situation, as fate has already made it for us. What's really going to boil our noodles is that this methodology for decision-making or lack thereof is actually the cowardly way out. To make matters worse, we may not even want to acknowledge or realize that we're too cowardly to admit that we were taking the cowardly way out. This is a less than fortunate personal disposition. However, all is not lost. We can change. If we recognize the opportunity in time, but only can we change, but we can then realize that we have the power to make the correct decision all along, we need to turn to our all-knowing Heavenly help. There is a notion, and idea surrounding circles of singles, that we will always be a better person in a single status, than we ever were in an unhappy marriage. I can't help but think this is true, having experienced both, and in some perspectives all three. Meaning when I thought I was happy in my marriage, than that trickle down into unhappiness and marriage, which most would think trickles down into being unhappy single. When in reality, after you finally get over yourself when you are sad and single, you realize how good you have it as a happy single individual. Why? Because you and your world of misery will be behind you, as you will no longer be headed in the direction of revisiting your past. Never look back. That's not the direction you're headed.

Breaking Up: Round Two

I don't know if it's just in my personal experience when dating after being divorced, but the breaking up, or being broken up with, tends to somehow get easier. By "get easier", I mean easier to deal with and to cope with. I mean, let's face it, being divorced is the ultimate of breakups, isn't it? There is nothing quite like committing yourself both body and soul to someone, then having that same someone, in any designated amount of time, turn around and say: "Op! Just kidding, I meant until I mess up, or if/until *you* mess up, I don't want to even try and work things out with you.".

Yup, nothing quite like that. Emotionally, that can be and almost arguably is rock-bottom. As a result of hitting this emotional rock-bottom, it makes all other breakups and "breaking up with" so much the easier; And by "easier", I mean less painful. Breaking up with, or being broken up with will never be easy, and if it is easy, you might have a personal, or emotional, or mental problem. Or you just might be soulless. Either way the diagnosis is an enigma. If breaking up with people is easy for you, you just might be too guarded into self-preserved to like anyone, or allow yourself to like any one. That's another problem and chapter in and of itself! But, personality disorders and psychological issues are not the designs of this chapter. Nor is giving the appropriate and necessary parties the proper commendations for still feeling the different degrees of hurts, and emotional unrest, that inevitably follows after being broken up with or breaking up with someone. Again, this is specifically about the breakup, and both sides of it. For this first portion I want to emphasize the importance of being emotionally responsible, and emotionally mature when you are the one who is being broken up with. Allow me to first say that the initial basic human reaction is to react emotionally. This reactionary state is perfectly normal, but it is not always the best practice. Think about it, has anything good ever come from *reacting* emotionally to any emotionally evoking situation? The answer to that is a resounding "no". Often times breakups nowadays are performed via text messaging, or social media venues (I know, tacky, right?!) This is both a good thing and a bad thing, regardless of tact. The reason why it's a good thing, is that the person who is being broken up with can still experience the hurt and rejected emotions that follow being broken up with. If they have the emotional intelligence, and emotional discipline, they can quickly process those feelings, accept what has just transpired, take a deep breath, formulate a mature and emotionally responsible response, consider possible outcomes from your reply, and then ask yourself, how would I respond if I was receiving this message? At this emotional juncture, being honest with oneself is mission critical. Because if you can answer to yourself I would like or appreciate this response if I received it, then sending that message is an obvious choice. If we truly are honest with ourselves and after we proofread the message we are replying to, we will get a response that will likely surprise (in a good way) the person who is doing the breaking up. Now, I will never presume to tell anybody that breaking up with someone is easy to do in any degree. That is simply an untruth, and you couldn't take me seriously after such an audacious claim. What I have found to be very helpful in my own being "broken up with" process, is to embrace what just happened in that exact moment. Embracing its will obviously hurt, but you're already in pain. So man up, or woman up and accept it. Why should you surrender your feelings so soon? Because the other person has already made up their mind to break up with you. There's precious little you can do or say to convince them to change their mind. Even if you somehow could do that, you've either manipulated them, or given them some sort of guilt complex to be back in a relationship with you. Now ask yourself, do you really want to be in that kind of relationship? Do you really want to be with someone who, in the back of their mind, doesn't want to be with you? That's sounds symptomatic of codependency and masochism. What can be some best practices, we may ask? I have found to just let the moment pass. Not in a passive-aggressive disposition, per se, but more of an approach of letting the moment process through your body and emotions. It may feel something like tiny jarring shockwaves that for one reason or another, can start at your fingertips, then surge and even crescendo as it reaches your torso and shoots to your other extremities. This gentle, but firm "emotional shockwave", (when you've let it pass, and then subsequently allow it to process in your mind) is like the proverbial bandage that needs to be ripped off. After the wound has healed enough and the only the remaining scar shows. I cannot tell you how soon (or late) this emotional shockwave will complete its reverberation, but I can tell you that it will, in one form or another. It all depends on how our tender or desensitized (or, somehow, *both*) "scarred psyche" reacts and responds to these types of instances. Oh, the breakups on both sides are going to happen. That certainty is about as sure as death and taxes. The quicker we let the process register, embrace and then discharge through our emotions and our psyche, the better. Now, unfortunately, there are those of us who may demonstrate a form of masochism and may not even be aware of it. Some of us like to hold on to our negative emotions like a toddler death-grips their stuffed teddy bear or dolly. Each of us has our own reasons for doing this. Some of us just plain old don't know how to let go. That alone can be reason enough to experience the sadness, the heartbreak and despair rather than feeling nothing at all, at the expense of feeling *something*. Whether it's negative or positive, however, in this example, feeling something negative is the emotional "safety net" that those of us hide under, as it were, as a form of emotional protection, or to fill the need of self-preservation. The problem is, we somehow fool ourselves into thinking that this will actually work. When fact, it will not. It's about the same as trying to keep warm on a cold night using a blanket with several holes in it. It may provide some form of functionality, but it will never be adequate for what we need to do, or should do. Ergo the problem we stumble into when we choose to isolate ourselves, and almost purposefully refrain from seeking help through friends, solstice to family, or better yet professional help.

If someone can show me an easy breakup, but I'll show you one or two individuals that weren't really emotionally invested in the relationship to start with. That's why, if we dissect, and examined the actual word "breakup", we will find a number of very insightful meanings and definitions. In order for something to officially be "broken up", or more literally, "broken apart" has to be whole at some point. Two independent, and autonomous persons, share one thing, a relationship. In this relationship, only two things can possibly happen. Either the couple mutually and in a joint effort, builds upon, and strengthen their relationship, and continues on that path doing that repeatedly, even past wedding bells and nuptials. Or, one of the two persons in said relationship, either lose interest, were not as emotionally invested in the first place, saw too many signs of "trouble ahead", or just plain didn't/don't have the fortitude to be in a healthy relationship in the first place. The relationship is never given a chance past that point. Now we will pepper this conversation with some logic. With all of that said, that doesn't necessarily mean that any and all relationships would work if they were just given the chance. There's no way I can believe that to be true. I personally am guilty of this and innocent of this at the same time! Sounds like an emotional "catch 22", eh? Such is the life of a mid-single. In any case, relationships, albeit healthy relationships all boil down to one common thread: compatibility. You can have two attracted people in the same coexisting sphere all you want. Attraction does not a successful relationship make! Sure, economical and familial backgrounds can help, and are certainly a good start and play a factor in the success of one's relationship. But nothing can replace or be as effective in bonding, building upon, connecting, and maintaining that all too elusive "spark".

But when one of those persons in this relationship doesn't feel that connection, doesn't feel that spark, or doesn't feel that the commonalities and the compatibility is enough to want them to move forward to a more serious commitment, then it's over. All it takes is one. That's all it ever takes. That's why I feel that so many relationships hang by a thread, or have already snapped. The problem a lot of us face nowadays in this dating pool, is that many of us aren't actually dating with purpose. We are looking for a connection, and compatibility, but the first "out" that we can either rationalize or justify ending a potential relationship ruins everything. I get it, we are all for the most part pretty scared of commitment, of letting go, and letting love in our lives, and even putting ourselves and our families at risk. There's a lot at risk that needs to be factored in, especially if we have children in our personal mathematical equation of love. These misnomers, and variables, can be more "exponents" than they are anything else (and yes, I am comparing relationships and dating to a mathematical formula and/or equation. I just try to make this fun for mathematicians as well!)! And like any other mathematical equation, when you factor in the emotional component involved, it generally becomes AP calculus, and while some of us can handle that type of complexity, for the large majority of us that are happy with our algebraic approach to relationships. In the meantime, the basic arithmetic of relationships is, for the most part, is unnecessarily complex. The breakup portion of it is likely the most exhausting component, as it usually requires the most energy, output, and emotional fortitude. The early stages of liking someone, or as I affectionately refer to it as the "thrill of attraction", is easy. Sure, it may start off with physical attraction for guys mainly, and the sense of an emotional connection for the women. Then the subsequent dating, courting, finding out all of the commonalities, and compatibilities that the two of you share. And that's when things start to get exciting. That part is easy! And then, in real time, right before our eyes, we then witness the blossoming of what could be an actual, tangible yet abstract relationship. We will elaborate on this topic in another chapter. With that information, I'm posturing my conclusion. Considering all the emotions, efforts, and energies that assimilate into the grand totality of a blossoming relationship *is, is* what gives the titanic and powerful force of the break up the influence it can have in some cases. All the while, we have to maintain our posture, dignity, emotional intelligence, wherewithal, (just to name a few) when that proverbial breakup hammer hits. Because, it will. It *so* will. Just don't lose your head over it a very wise and observant friend of mine once said: "you cannot say the wrong things to the right person". If it's meant to be, and supposed to be, it will happen. There's no sense in getting upset at the universe over that fact. Sure it's frustrating that we have to start all over at square one with somebody totally new. Yes, of course there's a lot of time, efforts, and emotions they going to dating. Everyone knows that, and everyone recognizes that already. It's not the first breakup we've ever had, and certainly won't be the last. Just hold on hope that you will endure your last breakup eventually. We won't know it's our last breakup until we find ourselves getting married to the next and last person. Because that next person is the one who is going to be ours.

Lonely or Being Alone?

I will never believe the dogma that people are meant to be alone, or even that certain people are meant to be alone. Maybe it's just the hopeless romantic in me, or the glaring statistic that there are more women than men tells me that no man is meant to be alone. As I've said before and I'll say it again, the Lord isn't going to let us down in the most important decision we have to make. We may not see it, understand it, or even believe it for some time. But then again, we're not meant to. With all that happens in this fallen sphere, I have to believe that there is something better out there for everyone. There's just too much negativity, too much hate, too much spite, overall, this just too much ungodliness for there to *not* be an opposition to evil. Granted, any evil or discontent is considered ungodliness; we just can't ever fall victim to all those diabolically-influenced devices. When that time comes, when we are blessed enough to find someone that we can and do actually care about, it's important to nurture that relationship, cultivate the good in our relationship, and to avoid any sabotaging actions. Some may ask why would we sabotage a relationship with someone we care about. To which I counter with it happens all the time! Worst part is, it can, and often is subconscious, and unintentional. We may not even know that were doing it. Faultfinding, nitpicking, degrading, insulting, in a sense, and emotionally distancing ourselves from someone, so they cannot become close to us in any way. In almost every case, these negative acts are and can be chalked up to "the little things". One of my favorite stories about this principle is called the parable of the grapefruit. Over a number of years, a husband and a wife wake up every morning to essentially the same routine. When the husband sat down for breakfast, he would sit down to a grapefruit. Always cut it up in the same way, he always ate it the same way. Over time, this became an irritation to his dear wife. He didn't know this at the time, because she never voiced her concern to him about the matter. Finally, one day, it happened. She was in the kitchen going through her regular morning routine, and she snapped at her husband about his grapefruit, and the way he was eating it. It was unclear exactly how her husband ate the grapefruit had that caused her to have this outburst. As the parable continues, she, with a relatively elevated voice asked him why he always ate the grapefruit in this certain way. This bothered her so much she insisted that he give her an answer. And so he did. He simply shared with her that is how his father or mother had showed he and his siblings how to eat a grapefruit. His wife, then realizing the insignificance of the situation, then turned the question around on him. In a frustrated sigh, she posed the question, "Alright, there must be something that I do that bothers you or get on your nerves, let me have it…!" Her husband then sunk his spoon into his grapefruit, and sat back in his chair to think. After a moment or two had passed, he just looked at his wife, with his big adoring eyes, and said: "I never have paid enough attention to any of your habits that might bother me. I've always just loved you for you." The wife's humiliation could not be overstated. To expound any further on the lesson that was taught that day between a loving husband and his dear wife is unnecessary. But I will share this comment: it's always a "relationship best practice" to let the little things go. Because little things, are just that! "little things". No matter how costumed, or made up, these little things may and will present themselves, it's never worth it to damage or afflict your relationship as a result of pointing out some minor flaw that you perceive your partner to have. No one deserves to walk on egg shells in a relationship!

Constantly pointing out problems that maybe and are affecting the relationship is the same as pointing at your spouse/loved one and saying: "your side of the boat is sinking".

Hello!? Last I checked you guys were in the same boat together! Even if you can't let go of all these little things, please remember one profound, yet simple truth, very few things are worse than being all alone. No matter how many people you may be around. There is this self-inflated idea that it's easier to be on your own. At least, that's what the adversary would have you think. Sure there may be some benefits and luxuries that are allowed when you don't have someone else in the relationship to answer to. But the give-and-take is so much more in favor of being in a relationship, than will ever be in being alone. One of the primary reasons this is, is because a lot of us are afraid. We may not readily, or even seemingly show it, but different degrees of fear is in all of us. This can be simplified down to personal accountability. We are afraid because if we fail, we only have ourselves to blame. A lot of us, married or not, don't want to answer to ourselves or other interested parties if we do fail. I mean think about it, how could we possibly look at ourselves in the mirror and be happy with whom we see? Failing family members, and friends, can offer some flexibility with forgiveness, depending on the severity of the outcome. If we are really honest with ourselves, letting ourselves down is one of the harshest realities will ever have to face! Relationships are scary! But they are also beautiful. The fact we all need to embrace and get used to. Because it requires change. That's why relationships are intended to be in adult situations, presumably handled by mature adults! Obviously, that is not always the case, but more often than not, relationships don't need to be so daunting, so hard. Anyone that's ever tried and failed and tried again and failed again, in relationships know that there are no magical fixes! There are no secret antidotes, there are no fairy godmothers to swoop down and fix everything with the wave of a magic wand. So the encouragement and motivation remains. Get off your duff, and do the work! Work like there is someone or something always trying to attack and tear apart your relationship, because there really is! Every relationship is under attack by a dark force that wants us to fail! They want so badly to win at any cost, personal, emotional, and even spiritual. That dark force is the sorest losers. The worst of any kind! It laughs at our failures, dances because our missed opportunities, and celebrates with every ruined opportunity to strengthen our relationships. Relationships are always going to be high risk high reward! If they were any other way, there would never be so much at stake. Considering our happiness and the happiness of another person, and to elevated levels the happiness of other families and parties involved. There really is a lot more at stake than meets the eye! Best news is, we have divine help. Someone that can see the end from the beginning, warn us of pending danger, and prompting us to act on opportunities that will strengthen and build upon and develop our relationships. This divine power, knows better than any of us that anything worth having, anything worth fighting for, anything that leads us to our divine potential, will never come easy! That's what makes it worth fighting for in the first place. We may never fully understand this at first, and maybe we're not meant to. If we were all supposed to understand and know everything about relationships going into a relationship, then we could never exercise faith. Relationships and marriage are a divine institution, ordained by God, as such, it seems imperative to include Him to the necessary and appropriate extent of our relationships. There we will find safety, there we will find shelter, there we will find the peace, stability, and fortitude to cultivate a divine relationship. One of my most preferred tactics for determining an outcome of any degree of importance is considering all possible outcomes. How better to do so, and plan for such, than to involve and plan with the One who has already seen it all?

Dating after Divorce

This title could be a book all unto itself. Contrastingly, this could possibly be one of the most entertaining, informative, and provocative chapters in this entire book. I will ask the gentlemen readers to pay strict attention to what I'm going to share. Now, I am of the belief and tradition that when one is given a blessing, and/or knowledge, nay even a gift, on a certain topic or multiple topics, the person and/or individual that is bestowed said knowledge, has a responsibility to share that knowledge with those who may not yet have it, or who may need a gentle reminder.

There are simple yet complex rules to dating women after you have been divorced, guys. These women are no longer in high school, and oftentimes not in college, many of them have their degrees, if not a few degrees. Many of them have life experiences and knowledge that exceed your own. Get used to this. Women nowadays in this dating criteria and category are autonomous, intelligent, sophisticated, humble yet very wise. Arrogant yet level headed, crazy as a bag full of cats, but sensible, and tender, loving and nurturing as true women of God should be. An important thing to know about women, guys, is that they worry; all the time. About anything and everything. If they have kids those worries are exponentially amplified. Their thoughts, their concerns, and their poor overburdened minds are running nonstop. This may be entirely a coincidence, but it's no surprise to me that in computers which as we know are able to process millions of functions and/or commands simultaneously, or in any given order, are termed as "motherboards". Now that may be an odd simile for some of you, but it is only intended to draw a comparison of a motherboard in a computer and it's multi-functioning execution abilities, to that of a mother's brain doing essentially the same thing. The point I'm getting at here is single women with or without children regardless of prior marital status, are incredible individuals. I once saw a humorous bumper sticker that read "The term 'working mom' is redundant." Truer words have never been spoken or sung! Now I preface this particular individual in the single man's dating pool because in order for us to appropriately and effectively date this type of prospect, we must know the individual we are dealing with as well as we can. Understanding and empathetic as we can, and perhaps most importantly, as patiently as we can. When I was first single after being divorced, I had what I thought was a legitimate fear at the time. As determined as I was to execute and finalize my divorce, and never look back, I couldn't help but also look towards at what I may or may not have to settle for. I had the legitimate fear that I may be, or pigeon-toed into marrying someone that was just "left over" from the remaining of the dating pool. This prospect nearly terrified me. And for some of you guys that are reading this, you are likely feeling exactly the same way! Feelings of needing or being required to (dare I say/suggest) "settle" galvanized me into dating shock. As a thinker, and a plotter, planner, and schemer, my brain was forced into looking ahead, and even game planning, for factors and variables in the soon-to-be dating scene I would find myself in, that I would absolutely have no control over or in any way foresee. Anyone that's ever planned or tried to conceive a course of action that had anything to do with your future survival knows how important every calculated step is, and how execution is mission-critical! What was so frustrating for me at first was that I was forced into this planning stage unprepared, without any prior knowledge, and worst of all no one to turn to that could relate to my very unique and unfortunate set of circumstances. I have full confidence that I could metaphorically dive into the dating pool, as it were, and the analogy of sink or swim with certainly come into play, and but as I had just gone through a divorce, my improvisational skills had already been sharpened and heightened to levels I was unfamiliar with, but also very proud of. Suffice it to say, I had confidence going into this dating scene knowing that I could respond and react as dating is very reactionary. I was also prepared that I was going to make mistakes; I was going to slip up. I was even going to disappoint myself with some certain failures, given my very clumsy and very awkward approach. But as certain events in my life have unfolded time and time again, I would find success in my failures. I haven't made it this far in life busting through my multiple failures without learning quickly from my many mistakes. As any true optimist would agree, no one really fails if there is a lesson learned, we just learn a lesson on how a certain trial or hardship isn't supposed to work. Failures are just stepping stones to the next accomplishment. To all of you men out there that share my same concerns and worries about prospects in the dating pool, you will most definitely be, as I was, overwhelmingly and very pleasantly surprised! Every single day, we walk around with, and associate with, attend church meetings with, and converse with some of the most competent, conversational, healthy (emotionally, spiritually and physically, and I'll also add ecumenically to my list of very appropriate adjectives) beautiful, attractive, capable, and affectionate women anywhere and everywhere! We men should consider ourselves so very lucky! Of my 6+ years of being single, I have been more than impressed with the caliber of women that I have met, built associations with, worked and served alongside with, and dated then at any time in my life in high school or college! Now that is not a slight against the women I knew in high school and college, that is simply not a fair comparison by any stretch. I'm simply comparing two entirely different genres, and two entirely different times by span of about 15 years. Women I went to high school and college with for the most part I would like to think are still married, and for good reason! They are and have always been and always will be high-quality and classy women. What I continue to be so surprised and impressed with, (and I use the term "surprised" loosely, women) is that in my assimilation, the remaining women currently in the dating pool, or that also experienced a divorce, should not, and most definitely cannot be regarded as "what's left over"! Just because one individual's, (male or female) proverbial number has not been called yet, is not a reflection on them as a person, the direction in life is going, or really any superficial judgments or criteria we can label someone with! These judgments and labels that we place on each other are so socially dangerous. We are creating negative dissensions which the scriptures constantly advise against. Inso doing that by jumping to these forgone conclusions we will literally miss out on too many high-quality associations and friendships. Simply because we were too lazy to actually take the time to get to know these people and become familiarized with their story!

So, men, how do we date these types of high-quality high-class women how do we prove these women that we are not the atypical knuckle-dragging, Neanderthal-male stereotype that current society may pegs us as? I have met some of you that, regretably, do match the description I just outlined. The good thing is, there is always hope for everyone. I am living proof of that! I was so socially awkward in elementary and junior high school that I began to take a very proactive approach of how to fit in, but more importantly how to fit in *my way*. To better explain what I mean by that is to more clearly define that all of us have it in us to be the best version of ourselves. We just had to *want it*. My methodology was simple and effective. I simply paid attention to the habits, tendencies, mannerisms, nuances, and neuroses of the men that had what I wanted. Then I made them mine. I'm not suggesting for a minute that we alter our personalities or change who we are. More like we're building an avatar after a character we want to emulate. Similarly like in a videogame when we are low on energy, or ammunition, or any vital aid to complete an objective.

We go through the motions to acquire what we want/need to progress and be prepared to win any contest. Speaking of video games, guys, I *beg* you to spend much less time playing these video games, and spend more time gaining social skills, intelligence, and quality, meaningful relationships with both genders, *especially* women! What is infinitely sad to me is how many women I've spoken to that have told me that their former husbands were more interested in playing the latest video games. Whether it be by themselves, or with their buddies, some fathers are reported to be spending much less time as a father, and even worse spending less and less time as a husband! Many of these women have made extra efforts to be attractive, to have attractive qualities, to be what they feel is your definition of attractive for sexy or heck even someone worthwhile to be with. "Gamers" as you are labeled, that play these video games almost incessantly are sending the very wrong and distorted message that video games are more important than the woman you have chosen to spend the rest of our lives with. It is heartbreaking in every sense of the word! None of your buddies really actually care at the end of the day how many bosses you defeated, or how many points you are ahead of them or a national or world ranking, or better yet, how many characteristics and talents you have added upon your digital character. Because, even if you were to brag to your buddies about these very shallow, hollow, cyber world meaningless accomplishments, sure they might care for five or six minutes or so, but then, the moment has passed. It's useless to try and make it relevant. Any claim to "cyber fame" is so short-lived, you'll have found yourself wasting so much time and effort and money, trying to chase something that can never be caught. There's no substitute for lost time. For any of you men that are so caught up in your video games and not to single out just the males, but you ladies to buy can be considered "avid gamers", It's time to make better choices with our time. I personally have one of the later gaming systems, but I only use it really for the exceptional Blu-ray, and my digital movie subscription. Hear me out, because I'm not going to mislead you and tell you that I've never played video games, because I most certainly have. I love all the classics! But when you are a grown man, with adult responsibilities, and children to father and parent, and a wife to be a husband to, everything else is and should be a very distant 2nd, 3rd, and 4th, on your growing list of priorities.

Guys, women will look for this when they ask you across the dinner table on a date if you are a "gamer". Some of them even know the terminologies better than I do because their significant other (in so many words) forced them to learn a gaming vernacular. They kinda had, to even though they had no interest in learning in the first place! Largely because they're too busy playing both mother and father, while their spouse had regressed back to their childhood years, playing video games for hours on end!

Again, it's important to have releases from reality, from work, even very temporarily from family responsibilities. It's what keeps us human; the mortality factor, very appropriately factors in to this equation. One of the more prominent questions that will come up again and again and again in your soon-to-be dating career, is that your dates will want to know to what extent you're going to be any form of a "familial and spousal liability". I feel for the most part, this answer is sought out not to find fault necessarily, but so the dating deductive reasoning can be applied here, and your date can rationalize and quantify if they want to pursue anything further with you. Did I mention the elevated level and platform of dating you men will be dealing with going into your new dating careers? I will say it again; with somehow even more emphasis on the reality, and the gravity of your situation. These women nowadays are a far more sophisticated, intelligent, worthwhile, and spiritual creatures than we men ever were familiar with in our high school and college years. In nearly every circumstance, you will be dating above you! I cannot overstate how underprepared most if not all of you will currently be, and consequently, how prepared you need to be in order to make any sort of worthwhile impression on these women.

Now, when you somehow get one of these women to consider dating you, for the most part they are going to be *women*. Meaning they're going to be emotionally-based creatures that also in turn react emotionally to several, if not every situation. For the most part they cannot help it, and because that's how they're made up. It's in their wiring and their biological circuitry. Now this is not a fault or a flaw. God made women this way on purpose. For us men to question, or doubt or even second-guess the way by which women were created, would in a sense be accusing God of making a mistake, which we know He has never done. What with that whole "being perfect" situation God has got going on (the author said, facetiously).

Be sensitive to their emotions. Women don't want to be told what to do. If they trust you enough to come to you and start telling you either about their day, or about one or more problems or difficulties they faced in a day, not only is this a huge compliment to you as it is a sign that she trusts you, but here's the secret guys: she just wants you to listen to her, hear her out. Empathize. Maybe even relate a little. A good example is the following dialogue:

Her: "Wow! Today was awful! I ran into this mega-cranky women inline at the grocery store, she saw that I was just in my sweats and a ponytail, and she shot me this dirty look, like "Ew, couldn't you at least have made yourself more presentable than respectable in public?" So I immediately became self-conscious on how I looked, which made me feel even worse for running behind my own schedule picking up the kids a little late from school…" etc., etc..

Typical idiot guy response: "Aw, that sucks. Hey, I only have three more levels until I beat my (enter ominous popular videogame title here) so… I'm going to go crank that out before you are done cooking dinner!"

Guys! *DON'T BE "THAT GUY"!* Seriously?! Your wife, employed or not, and in this example, we find a very busy housewife (nothing wrong with that, by the way) who is clearly super stressed about the failures of her day. In a sense, may be holding herself accountable to you — to let you know that she hasn't been sitting around the house all day watching her soaps and forgetting about any implied responsibilities with the kids or the house. She is choosing to come to you because she trusts you, and loves you, and wants you to feel involved in her life and in her day! So many times us guys overlook this fact because it becomes part of our "marital monotony". You know, the day-to-day things that us single persons forget about entirely. After so long of being divorced we may forget about what it's like to experience marital nuances that simply just become part of the daily grind and the usual routine. To let you in on one of the biggest secrets to a happy wife and on a much less serious note, happy girlfriend, is what *should have been* the following *response* from the guy in the previous example:

"Babe! I am so sorry to hear that! That sounds like you had a super tough day! I'm sure the lady in front of you was just having a bad day and had a lash out at somebody, and you happen to be in her wake! I'm sure was just a simple case of "wrong place at the wrong time!" Where are the rest of the groceries? Do you need any more help carrying them in? (Husband/BF brings in any remaining groceries) "Tell you what, love, you go relax, take some time for you, soak in the tub or lie down in the bedroom, I'll go take the kids to the park and that'll give you some good R&R time!"

Redemption.

Now guys, in her head she is loving you! But for some twisted reason, and maybe just because women chalk this up to being modest or self-sacrificing, but they will immediately say: "Oh, no, it's okay! I can handle this. But thank you, though!" Or something along those same lines. Be firm! Stand your ground! Women, especially mothers, are so used to self-sacrificing, the often times don't pay attention to their bodies needs and wants for relaxation, and emotional and mental peace. They have gotten so used to pushing themselves past their limits, sacrificing, forsaking, doing everything they've got so that kids know that they are loved and wanted and nurtured, they forget how to take care of themselves nearly to the point where they are progressing towards become the crazy cat lady! Okay, maybe that's a bit extreme! But my point remains. Guys, you basically have to insist that they go relax or do something that relaxes them whether be, oh, I don't know pick one of any infinite things women do for self-therapy. But I've done in the past that seem to have worked well was I will just call all the kids to the doorway, tell them to get jackets or coats (if necessary) and get ready to go to the park. Not only are the kids going to love this, but secretly your wife or girlfriend will as well. Take extra good care of her, and don't ever stop taking care of her. One of my all-time favorite quotes from Elder Neal A. Maxwell is as follows: "Serve them until you love them, then you will love to *serve* them!" As you can see, serving your spouse never stops. It is as they say "one eternal round". It's just like breathing, the moment you stop breathing, something is going to die. Service and love are the lifeblood of any relationship. But more importantly, relationships need to be properly and honestly motivated by love, compassion, forgiveness, and service, and *lots* of it.

Consider the alternative: the opposite of the godly attributes mentioned in the previous paragraph can be summed up by any number of negative adjectives. For this next example I'm going to use… (eenie, meeny, mieny, MO!) Misery. If you don't have love in your relationship or marriage, than the absence of love could most definitely mean misery. These persons can spread misery because they can't feel anything else. Sometimes they choose not to feel anything else. These people are also very good if not master manipulators. It's almost like they have to manipulate because they cannot handle any kind of real relationship. Those of us that have been on the receiving end of these persons misery by not "nipping in the bud" as it were, and truly addressing the issues (because there is almost always is more than one) we do the huge disservice of facilitating and enabling the other person's misery. The root of this misery can be any number of things. In the very serious event of a traumatizing abuse from an outside source, for instance, victims can often seek refuge in romantic fantasies with noticeably older companions. Victims of molestation learn to work the angles, and manipulate people so they can get what they want, meanwhile, undermining truth or morality (or in some cases, both) just as long as their own conceived or perceived utilitarianism is accomplished, and their own personal needs are met, or even exceeded in some cases.

Some persons immediate reaction to a miserable persons stimuli towards them varies on their emotional state, as well as emotional well-being. Everyone's initial impulse or perception about our attitude towards ex-spouses or ex-boyfriends or girlfriends is most likely that we dislike our ex's. Which isn't always true. Truth of it is, we loved them to the bitter end until the thought finally occurred to us that hurts a lot less to just not care. If you don't expect them to be affectionate towards you, then you're never disappointed. If you don't expect them to show up to important family events, you're not disappointed. If you don't expect them to apply traditional spousal care, concern, and overall spousal participation in your supposed life "together", then there are no disappointments. Then, finally, the switch inside your emotional faculties finally "flips". It's then you realize you've given them enough chances and even second chances. Enough hugs, enough of our attention and devotion, and then, we finally feel there is a king-sized emotional deficit that now exists in what used to be what was once mistaken as a marriage or relationship. By the time we finally realized that have given enough chances, enough opportunity to make good on their end, they've given us enough disappointments. Somehow makes the process of the emotional discharge possible. All that's left, all that remains is the residual sand and rust of septic memories.

Redefining My Next Relationship

We all want the relationship we currently don't have. This goes for those in the marital relationship, are currently engaged or otherwise affianced, and even casually dating. Maybe it's just me, but it occurs to me that most of us, if not all of us are "hopeless romantics" in one form or another. Alternatively, they can also apply to how each of us actually defines that term "hopeless romantic". Either way it's just a matter of semantics and syntax, respectively. In the same regard however, everyone's also the star of their own romantic comedy. Which, as irony would have it, our proverbial "casts" of contestants get "re-casted" as it seems, on a regular basis. Anyone that ever tells you that dating is easy is either selling something, or they are not doing it right. Dating most definitely means different things to different people. Dating can simply be one guy one girl going on, and accepting dates from multiple suitors. Dating to others also means that there is only one person they are focusing on and dating without giving themselves options or keeping options open. Neither of these really is wrong in any regard because everyone dates differently. Now, just because two people have different dating styles and/oor fashions doesn't make either one of them right or wrong. It just makes them different. As responsible adults we should be respectful of each other's different dating styles. So what exactly are the relationships that we want that we currently don't have? The relationship I want starts and ends with neither of us ever "keeping score", neither of us ever trying to story-top, or one-up the other, no emotional, or mental abuse. Yeah, that's a good start. Then a home and a friendship and relationship where neither is manipulated by the other, and comprehensively, at the end of the day, it never matters who is right, but rather, *what* is right. Where love and romance flows freely, and not recorded on some emotional checklist, or to be deposited in some emotional bank. It's actually a serious sign of dysfunction when couples start keeping score of anything and everything. Everyone has their own criteria of what they want in a relationship that they don't currently have. There are so many different scenarios it's almost impossible to quantify each of them. An interesting thing to note is that the relationship people wish they had is usually a very strong indicator of what they didn't have in their current or prior relationship or relationships in the past. That sometimes can be a common denominator with that one person. Maybe they just seem to attract that kind of person. Say that person has those deficiencies, but it's already too late. Registering in the mind too late because you're already emotionally involved after you have gone a few dates. During which time, you've harvested some physical and emotional and intellectual chemistry, and perhaps even some conversational chemistry. For those of us that are lucky enough we can find some intimate chemistry as well. Ever since I've understood the importance of different types of vital chemistries that should exist in a relationship, I've been on the lookout for the one individual, the one woman that syncs with all of the important chemistries. Now these important chemistries are very important to me. They may not be all that important to you, the reader. So let us examine these chemistries, you be the judge as to how important they may or may not be to you, and your next, and hopefully last relationship:

1) Emotional - this is a critical chemistry to have with your mate for several different reasons. It's not necessarily that the both of you understand each other's emotions perfectly. I don't know if that's even possible between a mortal man and woman. However there can be great steps taken towards wanting to learn and appreciate each other's emotions, but the quest for perfection and understanding emotions I believe will only be found and achieved, on a divine eternal level in the next life. Emotional chemistry as I want it, and understand it, is such a vital chemistry because it is quite rare for a man and a woman to connect on an emotional level in terms of emotional compatibility. The both of you have a certain undefinable understanding of the other, in terms of emotional voids that may exist, emotional strains that demonstrate in each other's day-to-day, and not only a want to fill those voids for the betterment of your companion, but because you feel a healthy responsibility to nurture and take care of each other's emotions and emotional needs. As it pertains to emotions, women are more than capable to use every shade, create with every brushstroke the pallet of emotions. All the while, we guys are content as a cucumber (forgive the simile) to stick with our stick-figures, and sometimes chew on our crayon's as it pertains to our emotions! Like most chemistries, in order for this emotional chemistry to thrive and be successful, it requires open and honest

and frequently communication. Men are not mind readers, we are not emotionally-based creatures, and women don't always (at least initially), think logically and analytically. It's because of these three components the men and women are such great compliments together. When we strive for the same endgame, leaning on each other's strengths, and countering each others weaknesses, ascending towards a successful relationship.

2) Mental Chemistry - This is not as easy to define as some may think. But I'll do my best to define it. However, keep in mind that most of these, if not all of these theories are not clinically defined. They are simply my observations, combined with a careful study of human behavior. These critical elements of chemistries, I personally have found in my own evaluation of my dating habits tendencies and patterns of behavior. Mental chemistry, at least for me is being on the same mental wavelength as the people you are in a relationship with four want to be in a relationship with. I am inclined to say that although there are plenty of intelligent, smart and capable men out there, it is been my personal experience that for the most part, women are more highly intelligent and mentally capable than we men give them credit for! Now, please understand that's not just lip service. While I do enjoy the company of my best friends and close circle of male friends, I love talking with and being in the company of women. The scope and range of their conversation is so emotionally-based and so fascinating, that if we guys were to spend 15 minutes or so just *listening* to them explaining their emotions, we would find ourselves better understanding why they feel what they feel, and better yet, not only want to understand, but help validate their feelings. I temporarily wandered into the "emotional" segment when I need to stay topical in the mental department. To have mental synchronization and mental chemistry with someone is such a rare find that it can easily compensate for any other shortness or lack of chemistries and other categories. People that are on the same mental wavelength and mental levels have a tendency of not only understanding better where each other are coming from, but most of the time they can recognize how rare it is to find such a person similar to them, and yet still so much fun to explore each other's mental facilities, all the while finding themselves connecting emotionally as their subconscious is attracted to their partners subconscious, subconsciously!

3) Intimate Chemistry - This is likely the easiest of all the chemistries to identify and relate to albeit too soon. Any two people that are attracted to each other can want for physical intimacy as far as kissing, touching, being affectionate, showing physical

interest by way of attraction. Where this is such a dangerous yet exciting chemistry is that intimacy has many different forms and faces. Intimate chemistry can come costumed, or "made-up" to look like real intimacy, and a true chemistry-founded connection. When, in reality, too much intimacy is experienced, and indulged in too quickly before a friendship level of trust and foundation can be established. Then, what once was thought to be an intimate connection, now has transformed into its diabolical counterfeit of "lust". One of my favorite authors named Henry Fairlie once wrote: "the lustful person will usually be found to have a terrible hollowness at the center of [their] life." In a different sentence, he states: "Lust is not interested in its partners, but only in the gratification of its own cravings… Lust dies at the next dawn, and when it returns in the evening, to search where it may, it is with its own past erased." (*The Seven Deadly Sins Today,* 175). Lust has so many deceitful faces, facets, dimensions, components and counterfeits that it's nearly impossible to identify them — until it's too late. This is why certain laws and commandments in Christianity are in place. They are there to act as the protector, guideline and shield against the many and diverse deceptions of lust. Now we've explored a little bit why intimate chemistry is important and we just summarized essentially why being mindful of intimacies counterfeits are so important to be aware of, because that's when the lines get blurry. It's so easy to look at our formerly married life if you are divorced, and try and think back on the intimacy that you experienced when that act can be properly experienced. At the same time, once that switch in your emotional center of your brain has been "flipped on", having experienced intimacy on its deepest and most physical in nature opportunities. It can be very hard to know where "too far" begins, and when certain safety zones are and can be compromised. Especially if two divorced persons are experiencing an innocent degree of intimacy and affection at the appropriate level, and both wonder how far is too far? This is definitely a case-by-case scenario, and should be discussed with ecclesiastical leadership, and other persons in leadership positions for should you feel you have questions. But in all honesty, the safest route will always be to listen very closely to the promptings and dictations of the spirit. Intimate chemistry might just be the most exciting and most pleasurable and most thrilling of all the chemistries! But it's also the quickest one to burn any potential relationship to the ground if mistreated, misused, and especially misappropriated.

4) Conversational chemistry – This particular chemistry is actually closely related to mental chemistry. It's most differentiating quality is the fact that two

mentally capable individuals can have all the proper and necessary mental capacity and facilities. However, if they don't have anything in common, or not enough things in common, or simply put just don't have any compatibility on any level, then conversation will suffer. Ergo communication will suffer, ergo the entire relationship is moot. Conversational chemistry is also equally critical because it allows for open communication that leads to further transparency and vulnerability in expressing feelings, emotions, proper intentions, and the eventual development of real love.

5) Familial Chemistry. Not only should in-laws make a sincere effort to get along, but more importantly, an extra concerted effort to blend families in each of the three possible scenarios: Dad/Husband with kids, Wife with no kids. Mom/Wife with kids and Father with none. And the "blended family" Both Dad/Father and the Mom/Wife have their kids. The atypical "His, hers and ours family". Blending families isn't easy, and it's definitely not impossible. There is an element of trust that is vital, especially if one blended parent is the only parent of the two that's "in charge" so to speak, when the other is away. A friend related the following story to me of how his former wife would be very passive-aggressive with child discipline. Allowing the kids "fight it out" whenever the issue of arguments/toy stealing, and or general "kid intermingling" would take effect that eventually. As to be expected, all the children involved would end up crying. Primarily because she (the parent) was blind to the fact that there was a need for general parental supervision. She never really got involved, or really "parented" until all the kids *were* crying. At this point in the progression, we're past the point of rationale and deductive reasoning. We're now left to do damage control, and "work in reverse" essentially. Instead of trying to uncover the proper line of questioning of what happened and why, *after* the fact the kids are crying, why only then is the parental figures only now getting involved? What the kids and obviously the family needs when attempting to blend is finding and relating to commonalities, and similar interests. It's really up to the parents how soon or late each other's kids meet. There should be an extensive amount of time shared between the kids to see how they're most likely going to interact with each other.

So, there it is. These examples of "chemistries" are all in a theory-type expression of experimentation and execution. Just because you the reader and someone, anyone else you are dating or want to date doesn't have all four of these chemistries simultaneously, doesn't mean your relationship is doomed to fail. Each one of these chemistries can beget the others. I likewise believe that these chemistries can be developed both quickly and slowly over time if the couple has the right intentions motivations, and are properly guided by their respective 'guts' and what their heart tells them. I understand that may sound very hopeless romantic of me, but to those who know me, it wouldn't be me if I didn't! I can be, from time to time, quite the undeterred hopeless romantic. It's what helps me keep "pen to paper" as it were.

When To Know To Let Go

This next chapter is not going to be easy. So much so that the thoughts themselves have already caused a couple of tears run down my face as I think about the forthcoming content, and the best way to broach this emotional subject. Tender thoughts and feelings have pricked my memory as I do my best to write content that relates to some of those who have walked this path alone. As alone as we may feel sometimes we are not really alone, not that alone however. We'll address that notion in a few paragraphs. Let me first share a glaring disclaimer with this very sensitive subject. Divorce is primarily about choice. It's the literal use of execution of one's agency. Most every single divorce or break up or both hinges on choice. There are external factors and stimuli that can influence our decisions and our agency to act. I believe it's because they are designed to do so. We have been created with our own autonomy, our own "light of Christ" as it were, and with the ability to make decisions on our own. That's precisely what divorce will cause us to do. To make the most important and belligerent decision that will have an impact, and emotional ripple effect for a very, very long time.

Husbands, if your wife has you contemplating a divorce due to her actions, etc. then the same scenario in the prior paragraph applies. Physical indulgences that are a detriment to marriages as well as God's laws, are not only diabolical in nature, but cause incalculable devastation to all affected parties. They also cause the numbing or desensitization of the soul. Physical indulgences only want their host to continue to gratify their craving. The problem is the more the cravings are gratified, as elder Maxwell once stated: "deadens the taste buds of the soul." (Neal A. Maxwell, 2001 October General Conference).

It's nearly impossible for spouses and partners to be brought to this point, and trying convince them to come back to the way things were originally, and weightings are meant to be. That's not to say that it can't happen, it obviously can. Agency will always be the biggest role player in this stage in mortality. I've seen it go both ways. I've seen and heard stories of spouses that are so in love with themselves and equally in love with their indulgences. With cravings ranging from lust, drug and alcohol abuse, social media addiction, any digital entertainment from video games to computer games, from neglect in jobs from spouses being too overly busy and neglectful of their husbandly and wifely duties, which also corresponds with father and mother responsibilities towards their children.

So with all this posturing, we've now come to the juncture of discussion. When to decide that it's time to end a relationship. Or to end a marriage. The me squeeze in one last disclaimer, that divorce is not as bad as it is made out to be. Of course divorce is, for all intents and purposes, the absolute last and worst case scenario for us adults wanting to be in a marital relationship. There are times, and sadly, more often than not, and more frequently than we would want, where it is time to cut all ties. Time to move on. Time to explore other relationship options with a spouse that's more in sync with our own marital and spiritual directives. One last comment before I dive into the "when". We should fight. We should fight for our spouses, for our beliefs, for our faith and fight for our families. As much as divorce is a very hasty decision, I'm saddened to say that often times divorces are reached and executed when an effort to save the marriage was never seriously undertaken by either, or both spouses. Thus =, the marriage and relationship was ended without really any real effort to save it in the first place. Not so much as even a mild whimper, in an effort to save what could've been, & what was supposed to be, and what started out as something divinely special.

You have days where you feel like the grieving never stops. It may take on different forms of tolerance, it may be easier to handle, govern, and maintain, but does it really ever go away? It's debatable. An argument can be made for both sides. Although grieving is natural and even healthy, it's best to take your grieving process in small doses, find distractions, healthy ones! Grieving should be like eating. A few small helpings here and there to satisfy the internal and emotional pain. I don't recommend sitting down to an entire grieving feast, metaphorically resembling Thanksgiving dinner. You can literally bite off more than you can chew! Also to be equally weary and even mortally aware of is the adversary's "sneak attack". He's always lurking inside self-pity-related emotions, waiting for us to lax our loyalties to ourselves! When we lower our "emotional guard" even for a moment, he pounces! He's ruthless, relentless, and merciless. The *literal* enemy of our souls, and he plays for keeps. Eternally, for keeps. Some of you might ask what some healthy distractions might be. Perfectly legitimate question. First, I would invite you to look inward. What are some of your hobbies and interests and things that you were not able to do, or never found the time to do? Me? I became more in touch with my inner wordsmith. I studied a lot of writing and styles of writing and dug in deep to the psychology of relationships. Does that mean I have the answers to everything? Absolutely not. Does that mean I have an opinion about everything? Absolutely! But in the wise words of my grandfather: Opinions are like butts, everybody has one and they generally all stink!"

So, explore yourself, meditate on that concept. What brings you peace, what brings you happiness, what calms your inner storm? Or what causes your inner storm to rage with passion? If any of these questions lead to the answer of getting vengeance or extracting sweet revenge on your former relationship partner, I vehemently invite you to draw your attention elsewhere. Connect with yourself. Take yourself out to movies all by yourself, go out to dinner all by yourself, walk in the park all by yourself. If you have kids, find a babysitter or have your parents or friends watch them for a short time. I am certainly not encouraging anyone to neglect their paternal or maternal responsibilities. I am simply encouraging people to connect with what's real within them. Listen to both heartbreaking love songs and powerful motivating songs! Because these songs help you to connect to what's real inside you! I will not mislead you and tell you this process is easy. It is not. This healing process is one that will take time, and patience. It will test you. It will test your sanity, it will test your emotional stability, it will test your mental wherewithal, it will test your spiritual aptitude. Every word in this book, and every emotion I personally have internal and external, I implore you to keep your eyes on the prize. What's that prize you ask? *You!* Bigger, better, faster, stronger, — you! What is my evidence and proof of this? For those of us that believe and revealed doctrine from a loving Heavenly Father, I invite you to study the words and Doctrine & Covenants section 58:

3) "Ye cannot behold with your natural eyes, for the present time, the design of your God concerning those things which shall come hereafter, and the glory which shall follow after much tribulation.

4) For after much tribulation come the blessings. Wherefore the day cometh that ye shall be crowned with much glory; the hour is not yet, but is nigh at hand."

Some days you're going to feel like you're a long shot to recovery. Some days you just don't have it in you, and that's fine! It's not possible to give everything you got every single day. Actually, I take that back, it's not always possible to match the same effort you gave yesterday or you're going to give tomorrow. I used to think that giving your best or giving 100% was a one-time thing. Life lessons have taught me otherwise! I have since learned that giving hundred percent or giving your best resets every single day I called the Cinderella affect every day we have the chance to do and be our best once we've given that best efforts as tired as we may be emotionally mentally and even physically, we can turn around the next day do the exact same thing. It's when you start excluding him/her from SOP's (Standard Operating Procedure) They notice this, every time. The demons responsible for ruining relationships and marriages - also notice this, and start to move in. Filling their heads with doubts, That's how it starts. They get more and more courageous, and more powerful with every step backward we take spiritually.

The mind and soul is the greatest trap of them all. So we've got to discipline and control our fears. The devil has designed his tactics to play tricks with our minds and hearts, if the Dark One gets enough power inside of our minds, he'll make us turn on ourselves, and turn on those around us. When you have the power and control of your agency, you don't need any other weapons.

Learn from my mistakes, for they are many. One of the reasons I even undertook to write such a book was to help other people *not* make the same mistakes I did.

The Devilish Relationship

Catchy title, eh? What isn't so catchy is the effects of said relationships. Well, I stand corrected. It can, and does go both ways. We mere mortals have a way of flinching, in a manner of speaking, and missing any number of moments. These moments that can change things in a life-altering way. I've experienced many instances in my life where good, better, and best moments have come and gone from my grasp. I've waived at some as they pass me by like a class I've never taken. On the moments that are specifically designed for us for a long term beneficial result, God has somehow made time slow down, essentially, grasped my attention, and prompted me to "pay attention" as it were, to these very special moments. Mainly so they *don't* pass me by. I of course retain my agency to choose to capitalize on these moments, or to let them slip through my fingers. My hope is that the ones that *have* slipped through, I'll be given another chance at them before it's too late. If not, maybe I'll be haunted by another prompting not taken. Maybe ignorance, after all, *is* bliss, and I'll simply be none the wiser. It is, for all intents and purposes, a moot point. The reason being is, the opportunities that get divinely handed to us we won't miss. How am I so sure? Because God has a very distinct, and unique way of reaching our attention, *exactly* when the moment is right. Now, just because we get these divine opportunities, doesn't necessarily mean that we can't somehow squander them. Mortals still makes mistakes, mortals still have his agency. That will eternally never change. It's the path we choose to take during our opportunities that determine both our blessings and our trials, and failures. That is the devilish relationship that lingers, almost hauntingly, like the ever-prowling persistence of the devil himself.

Two forces are ever-present in the universe. One that is good, wholesome, uplifting, generous, and loving. The other is malicious, destructive, envious, intolerant, and hateful. Even at our wisest age, we still may not have total command over our emotions. Why do I draw this comparison? Because even at our wisest, we stumble, we can sometimes allow our emotions have total control over how we act, and react. Once we experience any emotion that is any degree or color of hate and destruction, our patterns of behavior, and habits can latch on to that emotion and we can feed it and play host to it like a parasite and/or a virus. Like a parasite and/or virus, once our behavior is infected with any or all of those dark attributes, it may be too late for any metaphoric anesthesia, or antidote to inoculate our souls with any healing attempts. Or is it? Admittedly, it's so very easy to allow the devilish tendencies to confuse, and distort our spiritual barometer. Where we can easily lose track of not only who we are, but become so desensitized, that evil and devilish tendencies are such that we can adopt masochistic mindsets. We may even become such, that we actually *like and even love* the devilish sensations that are so anxious to cloud and distort our minds! Think about it. Almost all of us are guilty of this in one degree, or form or another. There were times (I now very regrettably admit) that I treated my ex so poorly as if I was her judge, jury and sentence-er (I don't want to use the term "executioner" as I've never wanted any mortal harm to come to her). Now, that's not to say that I didn't enjoy small kind of, may have, allegedly, unabashedly taken a liking to any of her suffering, or misfortune. For the record, this is not – I repeat – NOT a healthy mentality. We're venturing into the darkness with that kind of negativity. Revenge and deceit are not the Lord's way. To prove that point, both devilish dances are the exact *opposite* of charity, the pure love of Christ. Life is so much more than our trials. Some of the idiosyncrasies about divorce are enduring the mental and the emotional calisthenics to try and regain some form of sanity, starting with clarity. When you have these often-fleeting moments of clarity, a number of things can become apparent. They are riveting as much as they are diagnostic. When the clarity hits, you realize that you can use elements of your divorce, and the character traits you've developed, and emotional disciplines you've learned to make, or at least create your "Magnum Opus"! Maybe you wanted to be brave, and even be a pioneer of sorts and demonstrate that no one is impervious to divorce, because, more times than not, a lot of it depends on your former spouse's decisions, or perhaps you were the one that made decisions detrimental to your marriage/relationship. It's been my experience that people, family, friends, innocent bystanders even, don't often look at you like a person, or like a human even, but more of like a list, or series of "symptoms" that lead up to a divorce. It caused me to want to re-create a form of depersonalization, or to want to re-identify with the unreality of my status quo, wherein I didn't and couldn't believe that this was my life now, moving forward.

There are fewer things worse in this life and in human relationships than a loving a person who is never going to stop disappointing you. There is no version of this where either person comes out on top. Sometimes they can be so caught up in the "puzzle" that is their own life and emotions that they procrastinate to the relationships everlasting detriment. But they pay a hidden personal cost. They can become cowardly and reticent. So much so, that even with the fire beneath them is dancing dangerously at their feet. They can become afraid to make any important decision, until it's forced out of their hands. It's a passive-aggressive approach to any decision-making. They can spread misery so easily because they cannot feel anything else. They can manipulate people because they can't handle any real relationship, and we can sometimes enable that poor behavior.

Often times, we'll convince ourselves that we're better off being alone. Which is, in and of itself a lie and a tool of the adversary. "For it is not good for man to be alone" as we read in Genesis. There are too many benefits to being in a relationship, and a healthy, thriving one at that, by comparison to being alone. Sure there's more autonomy, but think about it, most every happy memory we have is being with our family, and being in a relationship. We may even applaud ourselves from getting over our trials (so to speak) and get on with your life, but in my head, I realized that my misplaced guilt was shutting down my ability to make good decisions, let alone any decisions. Maybe the perfect-for-me person is out there for us, but to some, it's not worth going through what it would take to find them. I personally don't subscribe to that thinking. I once heard a buddy venture that opinion, and it made me sad to think that the woman out there for him may just miss out on him, as it seemed for the foreseeable future, he didn't want to do what it would take to find her.

Further convincing ourselves that we don't need to be in a relationship is that we can feel like we're a "relationship freak". You may have different expressions and phrases that will replace mine and that's perfectly fine.

I'm choosing to define "freak" as the archaic definition goes: a whimsical quality or disposition. Why I use this specific term is, if used in the right mindset, it can be empowering. How so? First we need to ask ourselves how strong do we really want to be? Our attitude is the imagination's paintbrush! We are only limited by our creativity, and our own imagination. When I start seeing my divorce as a reward instead of a punishment, then I knew that I had suffered for long enough! Not only had I suffered enough, but suffered so that I was finally given a release! My whole perspective changed, I realized that I gave myself a chance finally, to give up on something that I knew I was wasting energy on. I was afraid, and I honestly sought the easiest way out in any situation I could. When I did my own personal inventory, I realized *why I did this*. Because, if I failed I had no one else to blame but myself! Life, and divorce, and life after divorce is scary! But, so is living in an unhealthy, emotionally, or mentally, and even worse, a physically abusive relationship. Get up and do the work! Don't be afraid to do hard things! Lesser people have gone through much worse and now, they're all the better for it! Because *nothing, I repeat, nothing* that is worth having comes easy! Divorce is *not* easy, nor is it comfortable. It's rough, it's tough and it will test your mettle and testimony. That's what trials are supposed to do! Sure I can pick up pieces of advice here and there, but me, I was going to make a stand! I was going to be the one that decides not only my fate, but also makes the choices that will lead me to my fate.

Marriage has lost its luster to our generation and has merely become a breakable commitment on paper. The shine is mostly off the apple. It's gotten to the point where we're basically saying to the other person "I will live with you and we will have a family until one of us messes up so bad *or* until we don't want to be committed anymore". It's embarrassing for us in this generation, really. Marriage no longer has much of its rich historic sanctity.

May I be so bold as to suggest that we all make a change. Make a return back to the way of traditional marital origins and treat the sanctity of marriage the way our ancestors regarded marriage. With the attitude that we choose our love, and love our choice unfailingly, and unconditionally. Unfortunately, there are more temptations today to break up a marriage than ever before. Some examples include money, video games, the complete and utter disregard of the opposite gender, obligations elsewhere. We are constantly bombarded with distractions from what's really, truly, and eternally important. It should really be no surprise. The one thing, rather, the one covenant that can return us to our Heavenly Father, is the one covenant the adversary is working around the clock to pollute, degrade, deride, corrupt, and distort. Families.

I'll never forget an experience I had while standing atop the in Trenton Battle Monument in Trenton, New Jersey while serving as a full-time missionary. It was a moment where, it seemed for a few flashes that time stood still. For this brief moment, it was as if the veil was pulled back from my mortal eyes, and the Eternal

Perspective became more and more clear. While I stared at the valley beneath me, what I saw would forever change *how* I saw, and now see the world ever more. The single thought that resonated in my mind like the reverberations of a tuning fork: "Look how the world went and got itself in one big hurry!" All of the unnecessary commotion, noise distractions, and deceitfully organized chaos, was and is meant specifically to distract, and divert the attention of man and men away from that which is eternally important. Our very own salvation. The precise reason we're placed in mortality. So that we all may choose – *freely choose* – to come unto God and His Beloved Son. They will not force us, they cannot, because that would be counterintuitive with the Plan of Happiness. What am I trying to say in relation to relationships and divorce with all of this? It would behoove us all to try with all the faith we have, to view this life and it's increasingly difficult situations with Gods perspective for us. The "Eye Of Faith" that all too elusive "Eternal Perspective". It's not easy. If we see our life and our trials and troubles only through our mortal eyes can make our much needed, and well-intended dependence on God so hard, and even unimaginable. He's there. He literally and spiritually stands at the door and knocks. It's up to us to let Him in.

How to Get Back to Good

Undertaking to write all that I have at this point, I will take one last liberty. I can make certain generalizations, nay even assumptions. Essentially, I can speak on behalf of certain circumstances and situations that I have either *never* been apart of, and only ever and heard, second or even third hand. These liberties I speak of range from the diabolical acts of adultery, drug abuse, physical and emotional abuse, to neglect, alienation of affection, and a whole myriad of abusive and destructive behavior. As such, the assumptions that I undertake are not without an antidote, a spiritual anesthesia, as it were. As with any gospel principle, we have to want it. We are entitled to every blessing under and in the celestial realm, but nothing is handed to us. Christs, and the Fathers full grace is *given* to us as a gift without the ability to ever fully deserve it. We are only entitled to the blessings of heaven when we follow the commandments and ordinances that are connected to the work we do for them. Thankfully, due to the ubiquitous Atonement, no one has thrown away their last chance. We all have heavenly help, support, and legions of ancestors on the other side cheering our progressive righteousness on!

Elder Patrick Kearon has a talk that has altered my life and attitude towards repentance forever. The talk is found in the 2010 General Conference in the Priesthood session titled: "Come Unto Me With Full Purpose In Heart, And I Will Heal You".

In this talk, he astutely addresses my first paragraph in like manner:

"I would like to share a message of comfort and healing with any of you who feels alone or forsaken, has lost peace of mind or heart, or feels that you have thrown away your last chance. Complete healing and peace can be found at the feet of the Savior... As I address you valiant young men, your father's, teachers, leaders, and friends... I testify from my own experience as a boy and as a man that disregarding what we know to be right, whether through laziness or rebelliousness, always brings undesirable and spiritually damaging consequences. When it comes to how we live the gospel, we must not respond with laziness or rebelliousness. As members of the Church of Jesus Christ and as bearers of the priesthood, we know the commandments and standards we have covenanted to uphold. When we choose another path from the one we know to be right, as taught by our parents and leaders and as confirmed to our own hearts by the Holy Ghost...We then seek to justify our lazy or rebellious behavior. We tell ourselves we're not really doing anything that wrong, that it doesn't really matter, and that nothing all that bad will result from letting go just a little from the iron rod. Perhaps we console ourselves with the thought that everyone else is doing it—or doing worse—and we won't be negatively affected anyway. We somehow convince ourselves that we are the exception to the rule and therefore immune to the consequences of breaking it. We refuse, sometimes willfully, to be exactly obedient and we hold back a portion of our hearts from the Lord, and then we get [spiritually] stung."

One of so many items and soul-indemnifying doctrines I love about Elder Kearon's statements is that deep down, in our heart of hearts parenthetically, if we're 100% honest with ourselves is that all along, though even the worst temptations and succumbing to them, we know what's right, and what we *should and shouldn't* be doing, and where we should be. The adversary only has as much power and influence over us and our God-given agency as we let him. Alternatively, the same is perfectly true about the portion of our agency can we give to the Lord. Are we where duty lay? Or are we gazing lustfully at the great and spacious building, or getting too caught up in the ways and enticings of the world?

Elder Kearon continues:

"The Anti-Nephi-Lehies in the Book of Mormon... were living in what the scriptures call "open rebellion against God." Their rebellious hearts sentenced them to live "in a state contrary to the nature of happiness" because they had "gone contrary to the nature of God.".... When they laid down their weapons of *rebellion,* they qualified themselves for the Lord's healing and peace, and so can we. The Savior assures, "If they harden not their hearts, and stiffen not their necks against me, they shall be converted, and *I will heal them.*"

You the reader, and I can accept His invitation to "return and repent, and come unto [Christ] with full purpose of heart, and I shall heal [you]." In this spiritually fallen state we can rationalize and justify almost any diabolical act. Even worse, like and then love to commit such acts. It's the slow and steady slippery slope to spiritual desensitization. However, we're not out of the ball park yet, so to speak.

Elder Kearon continues:

"Brethren, we find healing and relief only when we bring ourselves to the feet of the Great Physician, our Savior, Jesus Christ. We must lay down our weapons of rebellion (and we each know what they are). We must lay down our sin, vanity, and pride. We must give up our desires to follow the world and to be respected and lauded by the world. We must cease fighting against God and instead give our *whole hearts* to Him, holding nothing back. Then He can heal us. Then He can cleanse us from the venomous sting of sin. "For God sent not his Son into the world to condemn the world; but that the world through him might be saved."

President James E. Faust taught:

"When obedience becomes our goal, it is no longer an irritation; instead of a stumbling block, it becomes a building block.

"Our prophets and apostles, leaders and parents continually point out the track we must follow if we would avoid a destructive blast to our souls. They know the path that has been safely cleared of mines (or indeed scorpions), and they tirelessly invite us to follow behind them. There are so many devastating traps to entice us from the track. Straying into drugs, alcohol, pornography, or immoral behavior over the Internet or on a video game will head us straight toward an explosion. Deviating to the right or the left of the safetrack ahead of us, whether because of laziness or rebelliousness, can prove fatal to our spiritual lives. There are no exceptions to this rule. If we have strayed from the track, we can change, we can return, and we can recapture our joy and our inner peace. We will discover that returning to the track from which the land mines have been removed brings enormous relief. No one can find peace in a minefield."

No one has thrown away their last chance. All of us can change, all of us can come back. We can all claim mercy. Come unto the only One who can heal, and you will find peace.

My dearest readers, friends and fellow disciples, please for the love of the eternities and your families, if you have wandered away from the path of love and peace; it's so much easier to get on that peaceful path than you may think. There is too much at stake, too many blessings to be had, and too many hearts of the people that love you and want you to be happy. Not as the world defines happiness, but as the Savior has so clearly outlined. Follow the promptings you have felt. They mean more than just something, they mean *everything*!

Procrastination is the thief of time, and it is happy to steal from us at every turn we neglectfully give it! Once you are back within the "ninety- and nine" you will wish you had done so earlier. I promise you that, personally. Now go, and fight for yourself.

The Last Chapter

I have never written a book before. One of the few advantages I can see to that statement and action is that I'm allowed to get away with some unorthodox writing practices simply because I can. What I mean by that is, and yes, I agree I'm going about this in a very roundabout way of explaining, I'm staring at page 76 on my word processor, and I have just labeled my next chapter as The Last Chapter", when in fact, I know that it is not my *actual* last chapter. So writing ones last chapter in the middle of their composition is a curious gesture for someone like me, because it goes against what some might say is the proper order of things. I don't know how many authors, or lyricists, or musicians write their last verse as they are penning the chorus, but here I am, here and now, in the early stages of what allegedly is really is my last chapter of this book.

Now let's see where this takes us.

One of the most fascinating and riveting concepts about divorce is that it is both liberating and restricting. Often times people think they are eliminating a problem by getting a divorce. In nearly every case, we think we are legally and systematically filtering out a serious and or toxic problem that we are trying to eliminate. But, here's the dirty, dirty little secret: when we get a divorce, the only change that we making is that we are legally trading one difficult set of circumstances, for another set of difficult circumstances. These circumstances range from a misbehaving spouse, a strenuous financial situation, a physically or emotionally abusive situation, or perhaps its neglect of both familial and spousal responsibilities and obligations. It can be a garden-variety of things. These things are very real; especially in their present. We are *still* going to experience varying degrees of difficulty. Just like our parent's or those that cared for us (or both) stated to us over and over, life is just going to get more and more difficult. Because it will. It will almost always get harder before it will get easier. Anyone that tries to tell you otherwise is talking with too much sugar on their tongue, as it were. There are those of us that will take a more passive-aggressive approach. We'll rationalize that it is not "our fight" any longer. But, it is. It only ever will be forever our fight. We are just needing to attack from a different angle than before. That angle is mostly between us and the Lord as not every battle is the same. Ignoring the fight won't cause it to go away. Not only does that tactic delay our personal and immediate impact on the situations, but the longer we wait, the more ground the adversary gains on us. It doesn't end there however. The longer we delay, and every victory the adversary gains as a result, he grows stronger, and more resilient. In fact, if he had it his way, we would continue to do nothing at all! He wants us to continue to hide within our metaphorical walls of our own scarred psyche and wounded emotions. All the while he's assuring us that these walls provide some sort of shelter, some sort of emotional haven from his evil. To make matters worse, some of us buy into that. It literally shelters us away from the light, and love of our Heavenly Father. The darkness will just keep descending, if we continue to let it. Our agency is so profound, and so powerful, that our Heavenly Father's power and influence in our lives is only as powerful as we allow Him to be! Same goes for the adversary. We surrender our agency to whatever influence we offer it to. To this day, and throughout history, and evermore after in the future, the adversary can only operate within the boundaries that the Lord has set for him. While that may mean different things to different people, I personally understand that to mean that any circumstance, a trial that is given to us, at some point the adversary has to come to Heavenly Father, and Christ and petition them with a trial or temptation aimed at us. The Lord in His great infinite wisdom, love, and mercy, will allow these temptations and trials to occur. But Christ and God the Father set the criteria. They set the boundaries and the parameters. This is in harmony with the scripture that we will not be tempted above what we are able to handle. It is literally all up to us to choose. To succeed or fail. If, and only if we ask for it, with the intent to follow through, the Lord will bless us with inspiration and revelation pertinent to our trials and temptations. All the while, strengthening, and building us, our spirituality, and our divine character, the way He knows us and needs us to be! It's a wonder that we don't turn to Him more often for everything; for anything.

If we fail to turn to Him, by default, we subject ourselves to either our own limited devices, and/or the darkness. We will soon find that the evil will have become stronger than our will. Why not turn to an all-powerful Heavenly Father, who knows our needs before we ask? Consider that alternative: Lucifer's sole initiative, his primary objective was to take away our agency. Take our ability to choose, so that he could choose for us, and force us to be in his power, under his diabolical influence! All at the expense of Heavenly Father's glory. To this day, what blows my mind about that whole scenario is that *if* (really, *really* big *if* here) Lucifer had been chosen by the Father to be the Savior, to be the one to execute the Plan of Salvation to bring all of God's children back to exaltation, why did Lucifer set his own terms? Why did he arbitrarily choose his reward? Did he not think or factor in that such a deed of redeeming all of God's children would go un-blessed by Heavenly Father?! I digress. I am however thankful that Jesus Christ, the Son of God, did what no other person, divine or other was capable of doing, and did what He did so willingly, undaunted, and unflinching.

To restate my position for the final time, I do not necessarily advocate divorce. I do not feel that it is always the best solution to any set of marital problems, regardless of their degree of severity. I choose the word "solution" because the term "solution" implies a viable and situationally compliant endgame. Divorce isn't always, well *that*. It is, however, the best conclusion to a failed state. It is far better to live apart, void of abuse in all its varieties, than it is to endure a worsening relationship. It's true that divorce can be, and is the best solution to a certain set of difficult circumstances. But the decision to divorce should not only be amicable, but should be a last resort after all other venues have been explored, executed and exhausted. Couples should always refer back to their original reasons for getting married in the first place, and revisit the events that led up to the decision to get married. Having been there before, and crossing that very long and creaky bridge myself, it is never that easy. When I was in that position facing the dire prospect of ending my marriage, the simple gesture of sitting down, heart-to-heart, person-to-person, with the woman I covenanted to marry. Being nearly fully cognizant of the warpath that was about to become our wake. Dredging up the past that led us to this position of being married, seemed pointless. The gesture was noble in thought, but weak in action. What I have changed anything about how I went about a conversation like that? Of course. Hindsight unfortunately is always 20/20. I have often wondered if I was given the chance to take any of it back, would I? My mind trickles off into pie in the sky scenarios. Where everything continued to exist seamlessly and effortlessly in my marriage. I believe everyone that has had a divorce or a bad breakup has always imagined what it would be like if the marriage, or relationship, or both hadn't taken a turn for the worst. The truth of it is, I always saw it coming. I just deliberately chose to ignore the signs. There's a fateful twist that exists when you can see that diabolical freight train headed right at you. The things you love and appreciate the most are tied to its track, that emotional component of "fight or flight" kicks in. In those desperate moments, I needed to make a choice. A choice that, looking back on it, I was still petrified to make. I look back on the man that I was seven years ago, and my heart breaks. Mainly because I've tried to look at myself through patient and understanding eyes. It's never easy to do when your self-loathing. I think for the large majority of us we are all very critical and very harsh on ourselves and unnecessarily so. We most definitely need to cut ourselves some slack, give ourselves a break much more often, and recognize that even though it may feel like we're just going to the motions, were actually trying pretty dang hard! Success rarely comes in the first, second, or even third tries, but more often than not on the persistence of trying. My "seven years ago-self" didn't quit, didn't stop trying, and pushed with all the energy of the soul to right the ship, and better the situation. Going back to that noble in thought, weak in action statement, I realize now that although my actions were in fact my best efforts, however the results did not reflect my efforts or actions. There's only so much we can do on our end of the marriage that may or may not even affect, or have any effect, on the other person involved in our marriage. A number of dear friends of mine that are, or were also divorced, have all essentially said the same thing about their partner's betrayals. Their ex spouses all needed to believe that their ex's had bad enough problems, so that their betrayal had the illusion of nobility.

At the heart of the matter, and at the end of the day, a happy, successful marriage, is based on two people, willing to forgive. Willing to be overly patient, to love despite difficult or even impossible circumstances. Not just not willing to give up on the other person even when society, or the adversary begs us to. The adversary only ever wants to see failure. Doing so translates to him that he's winning. Sure he may win a battle or two here and there, but he will never, ever, win the war. He knows this, but it will never stop him from gaining and acquiring as many casualties as he can! Because even though in the long run, he will never actually win anything in the eternal perspective of things, his only victory (if it can even be considered as such) is primarily based on how many people he can make miserable as much as he is. Seems like a very shallow, and hollow outcome. So what? He's changed a few minds. He has somehow convinced a small number of persons to follow him, and be equally miserable accompanied with the illusion of 'freedom'.

Then, to live life in the ultimate state of happiness, love, and peace, surrounded by family and loved ones forever. I think I totally get his disposition. I know I would be absolutely and eternally miserable too, if I were forever shut out of the only place where the family of my Heavenly Father, of whom I love and whom I miss, and my family here on earth resided.

What comes after "terrifying"? You get my point.

There are so many people, and so much energy dispelled in finding someone who almost is never the right person anyway, it shouldn't be so hard. But the reality of it is, that it is hard. It's no question, and no wonder why so many of us become emotionally "gun shy". That no matter how great of a person we happen to meet after a previous "dumpster fire" of a relationship, that the fear of being burned again always remains in the back of our mind. To be again deceived in any way, or any other self-preservation antics that we can justify. Ultimately, would lead to our further being limited as to the degree of our consummate happiness. Many of us strident souls are quick to claim happiness despite our single relationship status. Happiness is absolutely attainable being a single person, but equally to be avoided is the stagnant swamp of singlehood mediocrity, and singlehood complacency. The highest level and degree of happiness in mortality is in a happy & successful marital relationship. That's not just me giving you lip-service, that's modern-day revelation. I'm just the messenger.

Printed in the United States
By Bookmasters